Praise for *One Million Followers*

"Today, the online world is so cluttered that even truly great content often gets buried or ignored. The good news is that you can take control of your ability to reach a wide audience—and you can start today, with *One Million Followers*."

—**Katie Couric**

"When we needed help releasing a digital series that we knew could do so much good in the world, Brendan was the first person I called. I'm so happy he is writing a book and passing on his research and experience."

—**Justin Baldoni**, star of *Jane the Virgin*, producer of *My Last Days*, and cofounder and CEO of Wayfarer

"Brendan is an outlier in a crowded market. His strategies are easy to implement and will lead to massive success. Working with him opened my eyes to the power of his ideas. He's the best at what he does."

—**Luke Wahl**, executive producer at Sports Illustrated and Yahoo!

"Brendan has done what most people only dream of doing. We're so lucky he's sharing his secrets. This book is a must-read."

—**Julie Moran**, former cohost of *Entertainment Tonight*

"Brendan's success stories are all the more interesting as they relate to massive global brands like Taylor Swift, Rihanna, Jason Statham, Katie Couric, MTV, *Vice*, Lionsgate, and Yahoo! As a case study for this book he put his money where his mouth is and amassed one million real followers for himself with very little money over a very short amount of time. Testing and methodology are big parts of Brendan's success, and he's incredibly generous for sharing those aspects of his work with the world."

—**Greg Durkin**, CEO at Guts + Data, former senior vice president of marketing analytics at Warner Bros. Pictures

"While it may be true that no one can predict what content will go viral, there is a tried-and-true formula experts use to maximize reach and stand out from the rest—and it will work for you, too. Brendan Kane gives you all the tips, tools, and insider secrets you need to make that happen."

—**David Oh**, chief product officer at FabFitFun

"Brendan's focus on understanding how things work is infectious. His curiosity and knowledge will make you want to do better."
—LATHAM ARNESON, former vice president of digital marketing at Paramount Pictures

"Brendan Kane will guide you through the fog of social media and its strategic application like the seer he is."
—JON JASHNI, founder of Raintree Ventures, former president and chief creative officer of Legendary Entertainment where he oversaw the development and production of content such as *Kong: Skull Island*, *Warcraft*, *Godzilla*, *Lost in Space*, the Jackie Robinson biopic *42*, and *Pacific Rim*

"There's an insane amount of noise online today—and it's increasingly difficult to get your content, brand, or message across to the widest possible audience that matters to you. Unless you've read this book. Brendan's done an incredible job of distilling tips, tools, and insider info into actionable advice that's applicable for everyone."
—EAMONN CAREY, managing director at Techstars London

"Social Media is now a currency you can exchange for monetary gain or exposure. This book allows you to obtain the fundamentals from the greatest minds in the world. Hearing from the experts within each field to arm you with the nuggets you need for social media success!"
—JOIVAN WADE, founder of the Wall of Comedy and actor in *The First Purge*

"If you're looking for a book to help you make a real and lasting impact in the complicated and ever-changing world of social media . . . look no further. Practical, definitive, and easy to read. Brendan Kane has written the bible."
—KARIO SALEM, Emmy Award-winning screenwriter

"Brendan gets the value of paid media better than anyone I know. And the value of efficient paid being the new organic and what that really means. And how really good content needs the right ignition and the right platform underneath it to be successful."

—ERICK BROWNSTEIN, president and chief strategy officer at Shareability

"In this noisy world, winning a massive following may seem unrealistic. But by following the smart advice in *One Million Followers*, anyone can build a powerful and passionate fan base, starting now."

—DORIE CLARK, adjunct professor at Duke University's Fuqua School of Business and author of *Entrepreneurial You* and *Stand Out*

"Brendan gives masterful and practical strategies that will help you reach your social media goals and beyond. Whether you want to build a brand, sell a product, or become an influencer, there is wisdom here so you can do just that."

—ANTONY RANDALL, CEO and cofounder of EQ, and entertainment executive producer/director for more than thirty years, working alongside names such as Jay-Z, Lady Gaga, U2, and more

"I wish I had this book when I started my career as a video-director over a decade ago. I am extremely excited to apply what I learned from *One Million Followers* to my own social media platforms. Anyone who takes this book seriously and applies the lessons within is on the path to closer achieving their goals."

—PEDRO D. FLORES, CEO of CompA Productions

"Brendan was shockingly able to generate a million followers for our non-profit in less than fourteen days. I have never seen such rapid growth in social in my entire career."

—RICH GERMAN, founder and CEO of JV Insiders

ONE MILLION FOLLOWERS

HOW I BUILT A MASSIVE SOCIAL FOLLOWING IN 30 DAYS

Growth Hacks *for* Your Business, Your Message, *and*
Your Brand *from the* World's Greatest Minds

BRENDAN KANE

BenBella Books, Inc.
Dallas, TX

BenBella

BenBella Books, Inc.
10440 N. Central Expressway, Suite 800
Dallas, TX 75231
www.benbellabooks.com
Send feedback to feedback@benbellabooks.com

Printed in the United States of America
10 9 8 7 6 5 4 3 2

Library of Congress Cataloging-in-Publication Data
Names: Kane, Brendan Michael, 1968- author.
Title: One million followers : how I built a massive social following in 30
    days : growth hacks for your business, your message, and your brand from
    the world's greatest minds / Brendan Kane.
Description: Dallas, TX : BenBella Books, [2018] | Includes bibliographical
    references and index.
Identifiers: LCCN 2018018000 (print) | LCCN 2018029294 (ebook) | ISBN
    9781946885609 (electronic) | ISBN 9781946885371 (cloth : alk. paper)
Subjects: LCSH: Internet marketing. | Marketing—Technological innovations. |
    Social media.
Classification: LCC HF5415.1265 (ebook) | LCC HF5415.1265 .K3595 2018 (print)
    | DDC 658.8/72—dc23
LC record available at https://lccn.loc.gov/2018018000

Copyediting by Miki Alexandra Caputo
Proofreading by Greg Teague and Sarah Vostok
Indexing by WordCo Indexing Services, Inc.
Text design and composition by Silver Feather Design
Cover design by Pete Garceau
Cover image © iStock
Printed by Lake Book Manufacturing

Distributed to the trade by Two Rivers Distribution, an Ingram brand
www.tworiversdistribution.com

Special discounts for bulk sales (minimum of 25 copies) are
available. Please contact bulkorders@benbellabooks.com.

To those with talent, intellect, and a pure heart whose voices are being suppressed or ignored. May this book be your guide to amplifying your voice, finding your power, and making a positive impact on the world.

CONTENTS

BE HEARD

You were built to live the dream you have inside.
Every person on this earth has a gift.
Dreams are your guide.

Do you have the courage to grab your dream?
I know you do.
I see you ready to beam.
To have a positive, lasting, meaningful impact on the world,
you just need a plan.

Use social media to your advantage.
Powerful messages and products you must share, the time has come,
no more excuses.

You can truly transform the world with your message and content,
It's not out of your reach,
my friend Brendan Kane's book will deliver and teach.

No matter where in the world you are—
the US, Mexico, Brazil, Australia, India, England, and beyond—
the powerful geniuses in this book will give you the tools—
the magic wand.

It's true!
I promise you.
Get inspired and follow your dreams.
Nothing's out of your reach,
even that which seems,
to be,
believe me.

Advice from the greatest marketing minds in the world are in this book.
They'll help you gain the strategies, partnerships, and opportunities
that you want to hook.
You'll have what you want and need
to be an entrepreneur and succeed.

These experts know how to get your messages out into the world,
and they share their knowledge with you.
After reading this book you'll have impactful digital strategies
and audience building techniques
to get your message out to the world and be one step closer to its
     transformation.

Whatever dream you have
. . . becoming a speaker, poet, model, social influencer, actor, start up
     tech company, retailer, comedian, or more, you can achieve it.
This book will help you believe it.

You're creative, independent, innovative, and have the ability to connect.
You just need the information that helps get credibility and trust,
which in today's society,
is a total must.

Take your gifts and turn them into dreams
the info is here
so get clear.

I have faith in you,
read this book,
follow its pearls, and watch your dreams come true.
It's necessary, valuable, and will absolutely help you.

If you attend to your dreams,
there's no telling what you can achieve.
You want my advice?
Start reading this book now and absorb as much knowledge as possible.

Dive in and get wiser.
Take your gifts and learn how to prosper
by leveraging social media to transform the world.

There's no one like you,
you can't be replaced.
So come out of hiding and let yourself be known.

—PRINCE EA

INTRODUCTION

THE IMPACT OF GAINING ONE MILLION FOLLOWERS AROUND THE WORLD

I f you have something to offer—whether your talents are related to music, art, acting, sports, or even building a brand or start-up— and you know how to leverage digital and social platforms, you can reach millions, if not hundreds of millions, of people around the world in no time. It's how social influencers have taken off and in some cases even become bigger than mainstream celebrities in just a matter of years. They started at home by turning on a camera and speaking to it, sharing what it is that makes them unique. With the right strategies, nearly anyone can build a massive global audience.

Justin Bieber is a perfect example of someone who intuitively mastered the power of digital media. He started off creating videos of himself on YouTube, covering songs that were already popular at the time and today is one of the biggest stars on the planet. He didn't have to do anything especially innovative. He saw an opportunity to capitalize on what was already working, and did it. Justin's magic was a combination of his singing talent, which moved people on an emotional level, and his ability to connect himself to songs that people were already searching for on the platform, which made him relevant to his audience.

He had a timely and emotional message that people resonated with and wanted to share. And because people helped him share this message, he got attention from producers, record labels, and managers that helped propel him to stardom. At one point, he even had both Justin Timberlake and Usher bidding and fighting over signing him. This was all because of his social media presence and his ability to get millions of people from around the world to view, engage with, and share his videos. He started off as just a talented unknown—not unlike many of you reading this book.

We all have things that make us unique and worthy of inspiring others. And I imagine that if you are reading this book, you're likely someone who believes you have something to offer and wants to make an impact. The main issue today, however, is that nearly *everyone* wants to make an impact, so it's harder than ever to be heard in our increasingly globalized society. There are more than sixty billion messages shared daily on mobile platforms alone. How the heck are you supposed to get people's attention and make them want to listen to you?

A lot of people think it's enough to just post or boost a message on Facebook, Instagram, or Snapchat. But it's not. You need to know what makes people want to share your message. When one person shares your message, your exposure and range grows exponentially—

it eventually reaches hundreds of their friends and can potentially reach their friends' friends as well. The velocity at which you get people to share your content dictates the success of your organic growth. This also means the more people sharing, the quicker you grow.

You need to learn how to maximize the potential of the masses to promote your brand or products for you—which is exactly what I will be covering, step-by-step, through tips and examples in this book. With more than ten years of experience as a digital and business strategist for celebrities, brands, and Fortune 500 corporations leveraging the global network and my expertise to aid clients in scaling, expanding, and accelerating their reach, I want to help you become an expert at getting people to care about what you have to say. Some people call me a growth hacker, to borrow Sean Ellis's term, but I consider myself a digital and business strategist. My mission is to help you reach your business and personal goals as quick as humanly possible. Most of the time this is achieved by helping clients maximize the potential of the content they have by getting others to share their content and brand for them, essentially hacking word-of-mouth sharing.

However, people have different goals, which is why, in researching and preparing for this book, I've reached out to my friends in the industry and the best growth minds in the world to break down each of their strategies as well. I want to give you the best information and techniques available to reach *your* specific goals. In this book, you'll have access to the top minds and experts for each aspect of social and digital growth. Whether you want to scale to a million followers on Facebook, grow a large following on YouTube or Instagram, or sell millions of dollars in products online, all the information is here, waiting for you to capitalize on it.

What I Learned from Working with Taylor Swift

Over the past few years I have focused heavily on content testing and optimization, analytics and data, and paid media to help celebrities, athletes, and media companies scale their reach and audience quickly. I've gone through years of experimentation and observation to get the kind of results I achieve now, but I believe it all goes back to what I learned while working with Taylor Swift. My time with her allowed me to learn the power of digital and social platforms and how to tap into it.

The fascinating thing about Taylor is that she built her brand, music, and stardom herself. She started with a simple Myspace page, where she built a platform that fostered a one-to-one connection with fans because she intuitively understood that this would accelerate her brand reach. She responded personally to each and every comment that she received on that platform. And any time she would get a request for an autograph or a photo she would comply.

Taylor once even did a thirteen-hour meet-and-greet session—which turned into seventeen hours—where she personally signed autographs for and took selfies with three thousand fans. She knew that every fan who stood and waited in line to receive an autograph or photo would be a fan—and brand advocate—for life. These brand advocates would spread and share her music and message with all their friends. Even though Taylor ended up physically meeting only three thousand people, she probably reached around a hundred thousand people that day. Each interaction she had was not limited to a single moment: fans would not only tell their friends about it but would also post images, autographs, and videos that they took at the event on their own social channels. The average Facebook user has 338 friends, so if each of her fans shared those images she could potentially reach up to 1,014,000 people. Fans would go out and spread the word for her. They'd tell all their friends and social connections, "I love Taylor Swift!" or "I just got this awesome photo or autograph."

Taylor still makes time for events like this. She attends fans' birthday parties, weddings, and bridal showers. In 2014 she showed up at a bunch of fans' houses with Christmas gifts and more than eighteen million people viewed the videos of the Christmas gift deliveries. In 2017 she invited select groups of fans to her homes in London, Los Angeles, Nashville, and Rhode Island for listening parties of her sixth studio album, *Reputation*. These kinds of events are Taylor's ways of giving back to her fans, while generating massive attention and interest.

This works for her because she's genuine. She doesn't just do this to manipulate the system. Not only is she smart, talented, and appreciative of her fans' time, she has a good heart. And it's this heart that has fostered brand loyalty, which grows like wildfire.

Yet Taylor can only be in so many places at once. In the beginning of her career she was living in Nashville. Although she could have an autograph signing and connect with three thousand fans in that location, she couldn't always make time for fans in other parts of the world. Her fans in New York, London, China, Hong Kong, India, and Japan were not able to connect with her. By focusing on her online presence, however, she could connect with people all around the world—and quickly.

Before meeting with my team, Taylor had spent around $75,000 to $150,000 on an all-Flash website that required two days to make a change every time she wanted to update it. When I looked at the analytics, people were spending less than thirty seconds on the website, and 90 percent of people were bouncing off the homepage as soon as they landed on it. I wanted Taylor to maximize the potential of her website, to go back to the fundamental idea behind her brand—one-to-one interactions. With the right strategy, she could leverage her website to foster stronger connections among her fans.

My pitch was that with the technology platform my team developed, we could build an entirely new site on spec for her in six hours. In a meeting, I showed her how we could dynamically change any element of the website in real time. She could change the background, move the navigation, change out the navigation, and control every element of that website, which gave her the power and creativity to constantly evolve how she wanted to express herself to fans. For example, every time she launched a new album, she could quickly redesign the entire website within minutes to match the aesthetic of the new album.

This ability to rapidly change the website allowed her to foster a more powerful connection with her fans by allowing her to express herself how she wanted, when she wanted, in the same way she was able to on Myspace early in her career. Over the course of two years, using the platform my team built along with some brilliant community-building technology platforms that we partnered with, we collectively took the time that fans spent on her website from less than thirty seconds to more than twenty-two minutes. How did we create such an uptick in time spent on her site? By giving fans a reason to stay there. We facilitated communication between the fans because we realized that Taylor herself could only talk to so many fans at once. So we built a community where fans could communicate *with each other* about their love for Taylor and her music.

We also built a system where fans could turn their Facebook profiles into Taylor Swift fan sites in less than sixty seconds. It automatically extracted fans' names and photos along with Taylor's photos and album covers so they could have their very own fan sites. The fan sites were built on the same technology platform we used in creating Taylor's website, so fans were able to customize and personalize all the elements of a fan site. Fans felt connected to Taylor, as if they were a part of her team—they could use the same platform that she was using and take any aspect of it and recreate it themselves. In a few months, more than thirty-five thousand fan sites were created using this platform. I don't have exact figures, but I'm sure this was a record for the most fan sites ever created for a specific artist at the time.

Witnessing how well fostering stronger connections with fans worked for Taylor's brand planted a seed in my head. I learned that if fans felt connected, they were willing to share content, messages, and products with everyone they knew. Once I realized the power of this, it became a critical part of my whole approach. I realized that you don't need to spend millions of dollars on marketing to reach the masses—you just have to get people to share your messages for you.

Not Everyone Can Be Taylor Swift—and That's OK

For as long as I can remember, I have always desired to connect with high-profile celebrities, executives, athletes, and entrepreneurs. I started off in film school. I loved movies and wanted to learn how to produce them and learn the business side of the entertainment industry.

I quickly realized that they teach you nothing about business in film school, so I figured the best way to learn about business is to start your own. The most cost-efficient way at the time, which still holds true today, was to start online businesses. So I started a few internet companies while I was going to college to really learn and experiment. When I moved out to Los Angeles in 2005 to pursue a career in film, the entertainment industry had reawakened to digital after the dot-com bust. I leveraged my knowledge in starting those companies to get my foot in the door and forge connections and projects. I ended up managing the digital divisions for two movie studios. In this capacity, I did everything from forming digital marketing campaigns, to finding ways to monetize film libraries, all the way to working directly with actors and directors on how to further syndicate their brand online.

Eventually, I wanted to branch out and become an entrepreneur myself. I tried my hand at technology, building digital platforms and licensing them to the likes of MTV/Viacom, Yahoo, Lionsgate, *Vice* Magazine, and MGM. From there, I dove into the world of paid media, helping build one of the largest social paid optimization firms in the world, managing close to $70 million a year in paid spend for Fortune 500 companies.

My diverse background has afforded me the opportunity to work on projects for some of the most notable names in the world— Taylor Swift, Jason Statham, Rihanna, Katie Couric, and the companies I mentioned above. Working with those giants has always fueled a curiosity and drive in me about what it takes to become successful, to become a star or a household name.

After ten years of helping celebrities, brands, and corporations grow big audiences, I started to wonder if my ideas and techniques could be applied to someone starting from scratch. So I came up with an experiment to determine whether a person who had never been on television, in a film, or in print could amass a large following around the world. The premise was that if I could do it for a no-name, then I could help *anyone* that had something to offer gain mass followers and exposure. I could help worthy people generate validation and credibility and bring them one step closer to achieving their dreams.

While pondering whom to select for this undertaking, I realized that I was actually the perfect candidate: I wasn't famous; have never been on television, in a film, or in print; and hadn't done anything (yet) that society deemed especially cool. I was just an ordinary guy who thought it would be fun to connect with people around the world. So in June 2017 I got to work on my little experiment. I put into practice everything I had learned from more than ten years of digital and social media experience to see how quickly I could get real people from around the world to follow my Facebook page.

To my amazement, by July—in less than a month—I had generated over one million followers in more than a hundred countries. I didn't know these people and they certainly didn't know me before this experiment. When I saw the number of page likes on my computer screen, I couldn't believe what was happening. It's not that I didn't know the numbers were possible—I had gotten this kind of engagement for my clients, but they were big celebrities and companies at the forefront of society. What surprised me was that I, Brendan Kane, a digital strategist who lives behind the scenes (or behind the screen) with essentially no platform, could become a public figure around the world. Suddenly, I was able to make a big impact in a short time.

The fact that I'm not a rock star, actor, or notable person in any way and was still able to get a million people from around the world to follow me is remarkable, strange, and powerful. It makes me feel a great sense of responsibility and has brought interesting new experiences into my life. I've received everything from messages saying how people love me or how I've inspired their lives to death threats and hate mail when I've shared political content that doesn't match some of my audience's worldviews.

But I *still* don't consider myself a celebrity or even an influencer—I literally built these followers in thirty days, which is very different from taking years to build them. I didn't do it to become famous but rather as a social experiment to see if it could be done and to understand the ultimate impact that it would have. I also did it precisely to share my experience and knowledge with all of you. If I were serious about being famous, I would have invested a tremendous amount of follow-up work to foster and build my brand and the connections with newly found followers. I want to stress that building a huge audience and cultivating real engaged fans takes a tremendous amount of time, energy, and work.

What it all boils down to is that if I could do it, *you* can do it. This book will teach you how. With these tools, you can set yourself up to be one step closer to making your dreams come true.

How to Achieve Your Career Aspirations ASAP

Recently I was working with an aspiring actress in Los Angeles. She's very talented but essentially an unknown with few credits. I asked her how auditions have been going and she explained that she had a general meeting with one of the top casting directors in Hollywood who told her that her showreel was great, and that she was an excellent actress, but that she would be doing herself, and the casting director, a huge favor if she could have tens of thousands of Twitter followers. Although a Twitter following has nothing to do with being a good actor, it would give her clout when the producers had to make a decision about whom to hire.

The value of a strong following doesn't only apply to unknowns. It remains valuable at the higher levels as well. *Game of Thrones'* Sophie Turner explains that she has been chosen for roles over better actresses because she has more followers. In an interview with *PORTER* magazine, she explains, "I auditioned for a project and it was between me and another girl who is a far better actress than I am, far better, but I had the followers, so I got the job. It's not right, but it is part of the movie industry now."[1]

And social media numbers aren't just desirable for individuals—they apply to brands as well. According to a Wharton business school study, social media popularity can demonstrate a start-up's ability to build its brand, integrate consumer feedback, and attract specific customer groups. Therefore, some investors take it into account when deciding what they will invest in.[2]

I've even seen how having a lot of fans has made a difference in my own life from a validation perspective. Since my numbers have

---

[1] Naomi Gordon, "Sophie Turner Says She Landed a Role over a 'Far Better Actress' Because She Had More Social Media Followers," *Esquire*, April 8, 2017, http://www.esquire.com/uk/culture/news/a16489/sophie-turner-role-better -actress-social-media.

[2] Fujie Jin, Andy Wu, and Lorin Hitt, "Social Is the New Financial: How Startup Social Media Activity Influences Funding Outcomes" (working paper, Wharton School, University of Pennsylvania, February 7, 2017), https://mackinstitute .wharton.upenn.edu/wp-content/uploads/2017/03/FP0331_WP_Feb2017.pdf.

increased, I've been able to leverage the influence for my own business. I've been able to secure more clients and partnerships. I was flown to Sweden to speak and run workshops at the IKEA global headquarters. I have secured speaking opportunities at events like Web Summit in Portugal, the largest tech conference in the world with seventy thousand attendees and speakers such as Al Gore, Elon Musk, Bono, Werner Vogels (chief technology officer and vice president of Amazon), and Dustin Moskovitz (cofounder of Facebook).

Social media numbers are becoming increasingly important and can have a huge effect on your ability to get in the door and build important partnerships. The good news is that you don't need to be a megastar to achieve growth. Just look at me—I am not on *Game of Thrones* or a talented singer. I basically started with little to no social following, which is exactly why I was compelled to write this book. I want to provide you with access to the best growth strategies regardless of your current level of influence (or lack thereof). Stick with this book until the end and rest assured you'll have a clear idea about how to rapidly achieve your career aspirations.

The Common Way

Before I came up with my system, some people (even beyond the outliers like Justin Bieber) figured out how to gain influence. This is great, but the problem is most people don't have a strategy behind their methods—and the ones who do have a strategy tend to keep it a secret. Those without a strategy simply try posting content hoping that it will catch on and go viral, and in rare cases some people get lucky. For most, however, it falls flat. Without a strategy, you're left playing with the hope that chance will carry you forward. And even if you are graced with good fate, using organic posting alone usually takes at least a few years to build a following. Frankly, most of us just don't have that kind of time to spare. The world moves quickly and we need to keep up with it so we can maximize the potential of our talents as soon as possible.

Because of the dizzying speed of the modern world, everyone wants quick results, leading many people to make use of paid media. They figure they can easily buy their fans' and customers' attention. They try to boost posts or leverage ads manager for Facebook and Instagram sponsored placements. Make no mistake, these tactics do play a part in my strategy, but those who use them without a solid plan never make the impact they're hoping for. Inevitably, it ends up being expensive and frustrating. They hit a wall by focusing on what they think is attractive rather than what will actually create emotional responses.

One of the brands I've worked with, Skechers, spent hundreds of thousands of dollars taking images and video content that worked in print and television and tried to simply repurpose them for social and digital platforms. Unfortunately, it's not quite that easy. Within just two weeks of working with Skechers, I helped them outperform thirteen years of combined social video engagement from all the Skechers Facebook pages combined. Imagine, if it's that hard for big brands, who have research teams helping them to figure this out, how can anyone expect to figure all this out on their own?

Probably because of this frustration, another tactic people have resorted to is buying fake fans. This is a practice I don't recommend because, well, it's shady and wrong. It could establish short-lived validation at a glance, but it's not sustainable. If people find out, it makes you look untrustworthy. And yes, people will know. There are so many ways to figure it out these days. It's not worth the risk of tarnishing your reputation. Besides, you won't really learn anything about your content, message, or gain the important information that helps you create lasting popularity and staying power.

Last but not least, the people I really like to help are the many who have invested hundreds, if not thousands, of dollars in taking online courses by social media "experts." Unfortunately, many of these courses are filled with fluff advice like "be genuine" or "be interesting." While those clichés may be true, they don't tell you *how* to do so. You're left needing a system that gives you the tools to discover how to be and do that yourself. That is precisely what I will share with you in this book.

The System I Developed

Beyond generating a one-to-one connection to quickly build fans and create messages that touch your audience emotionally, another cornerstone of my method is testing. In this book, you'll learn how to test to find the best strategies that get people to share your message. This is how you'll get fans in months instead of years.

By using my specific testing methodologies, and by intelligently leveraging paid media, you'll significantly grow and generate real numbers and validation quickly. You'll have a system that helps you learn what works and what doesn't. You'll walk away with important data that's useful for your business and brand development.

But before you read on, I want you to be forewarned that this is a system that does require you to work. And it's not just the work to build the followers, but more important, it's how you continue to keep them engaged as lifelong fans and brand advocates. You have to be prepared to go through trial and error, make changes, and, most important, fail. I never test only one variation of content; I test hundreds, even thousands, of variations. I will take the time to test as many variations as it takes to figure out what works. And you need to be prepared to do the same if you want to have success.

Besides, this is how anything great is created. The reason Facebook is so successful is because its model (and Silicon Valley's model in general) is based on the principle of "failing hard and failing fast." Some even say "fail faster" because that's the only way you learn. By testing, learning, failing, and underperforming, you will eventually succeed.

Too many people will spend too much time and money on a single piece of content. They'll invest all their resources in one image or video, share it online once, and expect it magically to work. Unfortunately, it often doesn't, and social messages move very fast—you don't have that kind of time to waste. I have worked with companies that have spent millions of dollars promoting a single piece of content that ends up falling flat and not engaging their core audiences. It's one of the main reasons I built this system. You have to test as many variations of a piece of content as you can against your core audiences and be willing to make modifications to those variations when messages are not well received. This is the hard truth. The only time this may not be necessary is if you are a creative genius like my friend and collaborator Prince Ea. He is a musician, poet, activist, speaker, director, and content creator who's generated over two billion views in the past two years. He can move content quickly and easily, but for the rest of us, which is 99.9 percent of the people in the world, we have to put in the time and test.

I'll walk you through the process of creating content hypotheses, A/B tests, content variations, headlines that attract attention, target groups, variations of target groups, test responses, and shareability strategies. An in-depth walk-through will take you through all these processes and more in the following chapters. You'll also learn wisdom from past client case studies and from my smartest partners.

What works will be different for each person reading this book. I don't believe in a one-size-fits-all model for digital strategy and growth. That's why I went out and interviewed the top minds in the world—I wanted not only to provide you with my strategy for growth but also with other options so you could choose what works best for you. Then, once you understand the strategies outlined and discussed in the following chapters, you'll have the ability to create your own model with lasting results. When you're done with this book you'll understand the best ways to leverage who and what you are to make an impact and to reach your goals as quickly as possible.

In this book, you'll find some of the top strategies and insights that will reshape the way individuals, brands, and companies build connections with their fans. You'll finally have a system that gives you the power to achieve your career goals and aspirations. For continued education beyond this book, please check out our video series at www.optin.tv or send me an email directly at b@optin.tv.

This process starts with understanding the ins and outs of content testing. Once you master this knowledge you'll be ten steps closer to having more fans and exposure for your content than the majority of people out there. So let's begin there, with the fundamental step of learning how to maximize the potential of your content and build fans fast.

CHAPTER 1

HOW I GAINED ONE MILLION FOLLOWERS

Although it may sound like a ludicrous undertaking, building a massive social following in thirty days or less is possible. But first I should point out that the real value of this chapter—and book—is not simply about how I generated a million followers. To be completely transparent, the way I generated a million followers involves using a growth hack, which I will explain in this chapter. But I don't want to promote the idea of relying too heavily on growth hacks. Of course they can help you, but without the other strategies, mind-sets, and processes shared in this book, you won't become a rock star at content creation. You may succeed at playing the numbers game, but you won't build a lasting presence. Ask anyone who has had digital success and they'll tell you without a doubt that *content* is the critical factor in growing and engaging large audiences. So keep that in mind as I explain how I gained a million followers.

The key to quickly scaling your following is an agile approach of producing, testing, and measuring how people respond to your content in real time. It's a great strategy for those who don't have three or four years to invest in building their platform because it gives you immediate validation and credibility to stand out right now. Building the audience is actually pretty easy. It's maintaining and engaging that audience that requires hard work over time.

You need to accept this fact before going in. You can get a lot of fans fast, but to have a thriving and lasting social media presence you need to understand the testing, messaging, and content strategies provided in the following chapters. They're filled with advice from the top minds around the world to scale large audiences and keep them engaged.

Three Phases to the Process

The foundation of my methodology for gaining one million followers consists of these three steps:

1. **HYPOTHESIZE.** Quickly identify a hypothesis of a format, story, or theme that engages audiences around a specific message.
2. **TEST.** Produce a low-cost proof of the concept or message that can be tested and validated and learn everything you can about what does and doesn't work from the results.
3. **PIVOT.** If the hypothesis is proved correct, invest in it further. If it's disproved, quickly repeat the process again with a new format, story, or theme.

Hypothesize, test, and pivot is your new mantra. The model is simple—the hard part is figuring out what to test and when to pivot.

You need to test many different variations that have a strong hook to catch and hold people's attention. Then, based on those tests, you figure out which variations yield the best results and keep investing in the ones that do. Or, if none of them are working, you need to pivot—go back, set a new hypothesis, and start the process over again.

When I was building a million followers, my core focus was on becoming recognized for thought leadership, since my true passion is speaking and teaching other people. As a digital and business strategist, I'm always testing as much content as possible to get an understanding of what does and doesn't work for clients, but when building my following I focused my brand around the themes of thought leadership, teaching, and inspirational posts.

One of my most interesting and successful experiments involved podcasts. I *hypothesized* that podcasting would be a great outlet for me as an individual because I'd learned a lot about them in my work with Katie Couric, which I'll speak about in the chapters to come. Suffice it to say, I'd seen that you could essentially "reverse engineer" podcasts for Facebook and scale audience and engagement quickly. We did this by cutting short audio clips from podcast interviews I had created with a few partners and celebrities and then turned them into a video by playing the audio over a still image or a slide show, or cutting it against stock video that represented what was being discussed. Running these videos through various tests, I found that I could reach millions of people in *days*—most of the top podcasts in the world don't even reach that in a month. The trick is, you don't have to reinvent the wheel. Look around and borrow ideas from other people's successes.

The podcast content I *tested* consisted of interviews with Justin Baldoni, lead actor in the TV show *Jane the Virgin*; Jeff King, an expert in the Process Communication Model (featured in chapter three); and Dr. Drew. I cut the interview audio into three styles of video posts: (1) videos showing a single image with the audio played over it, (2) videos showing multiple images with the audio played over it, and (3) videos with stock footage or clips I found online that matched the audio playing over it. Then I tested all those clips against each other to see which generated the most shareability and earned lift. For each interview, I cut anywhere between three and ten audio clips and created unique videos for each one. From there I generated anywhere between ten and a hundred variations of each clip (more later on how to scale variations of content quickly).

The best-performing content by far was one of the variations of the Justin Baldoni interview. It's an inspirational video in which he encourages people to live their best and most desired life. He also talks about how to make choices that will make your life happier and more fulfilling. I *learned* that the message of the content (that is expressed through the headline) was incredibly important, and that choosing the right one is an influential factor in getting people to click and share. I want to point out that I am against clickbait— the headline/hook point should always match the content. I also learned that the visuals were really important. A video with stock footage that represented the audio or actual video from the interview per-formed better than a single image. Moreover, using someone with a large following that you can target and tap into also helps garner attention—but not necessarily *engagement* if the content is not solid.

Additionally, I shared and tested a variety of inspirational quotes—I'd seen other people like Gary Vaynerchuk (an entrepre-neur with two and a half million followers) have a lot of success with these types of posts. Some of the quotes I tested came from people I admire like Steven Spielberg and Oprah, who share similar view-points to me. After seeing positive initial results, I switched my focus to creating my own personal quotes, which make up a good percentage of the posts I publish to my page today. I learned that quotes on images work extremely well because people like to interact visually and mentally with positive and inspirational content. An advantage of images over videos here is that it's much easier to create a high-quality image than a video. There are so many variables that go into making a great video: tone, pacing, the first three seconds, captions, title cards, length, and so forth. With a photo, on the other hand, you just have to choose the right photo with the right quote—fewer variables have to come together to make it successful.

The short-term strategy is to look at the tests and learn what works in real time. Those results inform you and dictate the content you'll produce on a weekly basis. Then, when you start seeing the macrotrends of what works, it informs your long-term content strategy, which you also need to check against your brand's overall message. For example, as an experiment I tested viral videos of pranks and of kittens and dogs doing funny things. Although they all performed really well, I decided to *pivot* because they didn't align with my brand's theme of thought leadership. Note that the type of content that resonates with your audience can change over time. Look at both your short-term and long-term content strategies, discover how they play into each other, and move toward what works.

Why My System Focuses on Facebook

Recently Facebook has been in the news related to concerns about how they use people's data. I want to address this topic and explain why I still choose to use Facebook and believe that it's a valuable platform. As Alexandra Samuel points out in her report on Cambridge Analytica in *The Verge*, the internet has been designed to capitalize on the free sharing of user data.[1] This won't change until businesses, consumers, and regulators decide to adopt a different model.

There's also a difference between using data to help people and using it to exploit them. Creating fake news (with malicious or manipulative intent) is irresponsible and not advisable to anyone. On the other hand, gathering data that allows marketers to know their customers' needs and better understand them can serve in providing value to potential customers.

In light of what's happened, there may be a need to change the way these systems and companies operate, especially in regard to their level of transparency. It will be interesting to see if a new agreement or model is created as a result. In the meantime, I advise you to engage with the data you use on Facebook responsibly and ethically, as I do in my practice.

As I mentioned, after working with celebrities like Taylor Swift, I learned that the number one key to success in scaling massive audiences is getting people to share your message for you. The more people share your content, the faster and more cost effectively you can scale your audience. I chose to build one million followers on Facebook because it's the most democratic and share-friendly platform, not to mention the easiest and quickest on which to scale and

---

[1] Alexandra Samuel, "The shady data-gathering tactics used by Cambridge Analytica were an open secret to online marketers. I know, because I was one," *The Verge*, March 25, 2018, https://www.theverge.com/2018/3/25/17161726/facebook-cambridge-analytica-data-online-marketers.

grow an audience (more on this below). In fact, Facebook is used to share content more than email or any other online social platform.[2] From my experience, experiments, and conversations with the greatest marketing and social media minds in the world, I've learned that if you have a great piece of content, people will rapidly share it on Facebook, maximizing the potential earned lift of your content.

Facebook lends itself more readily to scaling than other platforms because it was built around the concept of sharing. On other platforms, virality is much more based on SEO (search engine optimization) rankings and algorithms. Yes, there are algorithms at play on Facebook—I'll discuss these more in the next section—but if people share your content, you can overcome the algorithms much more easily than on platforms like YouTube, Snapchat, and Instagram. For example, filmmaker, speaker, and activist Prince Ea shares videos that get thirty million views on Facebook within the first week, which would be nearly impossible to achieve at this velocity on other platforms.

Another reason I recommend working with Facebook is that it's the largest platform. It gives you access to a community of more than two billion people (and rising).[3] Facebook's advertising platform (which also powers Instagram, WhatsApp, and Facebook Messenger) is an incredibly strong market research tool. You can use it to effectively test all kinds of content and see how they resonate with people from different backgrounds and in different parts of the

---

[2] Jeff Bullas, "Do People Share More on Facebook or Twitter?" *Jeff Bullas's Blog*, http://www.jeffbullas.com/do-people-share-more-on-facebook-or-twitter.

[3] Jeff Dunn, "Facebook totally dominates the list of most popular social media apps," *Business Insider*, July 27, 2017, http://www.businessinsider.com/facebook-dominates-most-popular-social-media-apps-chart-2017-7.

world. When analyzed correctly, this information gives you a lot of power to enhance your brand and understand your marketability.

Three Ways to Generate a Following

There are three ways you can grow a following on Facebook. The first two ways are by using the Facebook advertising platform, which enables you to (1) *make a piece of content go viral* to gain mass awareness with the correlative effect of people following you based on this exposure or (2) *use a page likes ad unit* (any ad with the goal of creating more likes/followers for your page) to target potential new followers. One of the simplest ways to create this type of campaign is to access it through Ads Manager on the Facebook ad platform and select Page Likes as your marketing goal/objective. This isn't the only way to use page likes ad units, however—explaining the nuances of the Facebook ad platform could be an entire book in and of itself.

> ▶ For more resources to assist you in learning how to use the Facebook ad platform, check out www.optin.tv/fbtutorials.

Both tactics above are effective, and ultimately I recommend using a combination of them. Knowing how to make a piece of content go viral is a stronger long-term tactic. Start by testing the content you already have and see if it results in a significant number of people sharing it. It's always best to generate followers with great viral content because that will keep your audience engaged. You may be asking yourself, "How do I go about creating shareable or viral content on a consistent basis? What's the formula?" Glad you asked—chapter five is entirely about this topic. But for now, it's still valuable to start by creating an ad with the marketing objective of "page likes," as I mentioned above, to test and learn what it takes to get someone to follow you.

Because of Facebook's algorithms, even after you hit a million followers, the content that you post will only reach on average between 2 and 5 percent of your audience. Most people have liked hundreds, if not thousands, of pages. When people look at their main feed, Facebook can only show them so much content. The main feed needs to be limited to the best-performing content from all the pages one has opted in to. And Facebook also makes sure that users are getting content from their closest friends. The algorithms weigh content to make sure that people's social feeds are filled with what interests them. If your content isn't resonating, it will only be shown to a small subset of your audience. On the other hand, if the content performs well, it'll reach a vast majority (if not all) of your following base, giving you the potential to get that content shared and to gain organic growth.

Keep this in mind if you choose to use the Facebook page like objective. It was part of my strategy in building my following because it's a great tool that can scale and build your validation number to a credible point. You gain real connections with real people, and your newfound credibility can be leveraged to fuel organic growth, which is the third way of gaining a following on Facebook. I'll get deeper into achieving organic growth in subsequent chapters—particularly through strategic alliances in chapter six—but you still need to build a solid content strategy via the first two methods so you don't limit yourself to only reaching 2 to 5 percent of your audience per post.

▶ For a more detailed explanation of how I used the page objective to scale quickly, visit www.optin.tv/brendan.

There's Always a CPA for Gaining Followers

Some influencers have gained fans by publishing content every day and building strong relationships with their audience over a significant period. They have a relationship with their fans—the fans know who they are and have been engaging with them over the course of years. Obviously, this isn't the best option to gain fast results. Which brings up an important consideration: *There's always a CPA (cost per acquisition) for a follower.* If you're building a fan base, even from an organic perspective there's a cost to acquire a follower or subscriber. Anyone who tells you that getting fans organically means gaining followers for free is wrong.

Top influencers like entrepreneur Gary Vaynerchuk often have a full-time staff working behind them. Vaynerchuk, who runs one of the top social agencies in the world, leverages the knowledge from all the work he does for clients to build his personal brand and vice versa. His agency not only supports his clients but also supports him in creating, editing, and marketing his content. However, if you're not paying to have a team behind you like Vaynerchuk, you're paying with your time by doing all the work—shooting, editing, posting, monitoring, and the like—yourself.

One of the reasons I chose to hypothesize, test, and pivot was because I didn't have access to a full team. I got to one million with minimal support. There was a cost associated with the media spend, but no matter which route you take there's a cost, whether in time, commitment, money, or a combination of all three. You have to invest to gain followers. My strategy just happens to be one of the quickest and requires the least number of people. Of course, that doesn't take away from the fact that you still have work to do once you've established the followers. It's not like you get to a million and you're done. You have to actually engage that audience, or else you lose your credibility.

How Much Money Do I Have to Invest?

My friend and former colleague David Oh, the chief product officer and head of growth at FabFitFun (a quarterly lifestyle subscription box for women that generates hundreds of millions of dollars a year in revenue), explains that many people believe that paid media is somehow irrelevant. He feels that when we reject the importance of paid media we reject the importance of consumers—a concept he finds dehumanizing. He doesn't know how people can expect to reach their audience without some form of advertising.

The key to making advertising advantageous, he shares, is being conscious about how much you spend on it and how much you'll get out of it. Looking at return on investment (ROI) is the most fundamental and important thing people forget when talking about marketing, business, and advertising. How much money did you spend and how much money did you get out of that investment? That's the only relevant question to ask. And sometimes what you get out of it isn't a dollar amount. Sometimes it's the credibility or the boost that having high social numbers and engagement can give you. Return on investment may come in the form of getting a TV job, into a film, a modeling contract, a record deal, or an investor for your start-up, but you need to ask yourself how much those connections are worth to you. What is the outcome you're looking for? And what amount of money or time are you willing to put in to get those results?

One of Hollywood's most successful movie producers, media executives, and investors, Jon Jashni backs up what Sophie Turner attested to in the intro and explains that studios pay attention to the level of social following and social engagement that specific actors have when making casting decisions. It's cheaper for studios to reach more people when actors have grown their social presence. This is especially true when casting television, which moves faster and requires more noise and urgency to get noticed. Jashni states, "If an actor's relative attractiveness and craftsmanship is equal, the thing that will tip decision making will be the social reach."

This is true in many industries today. Think about how much value your social numbers will provide and come up with a dollar amount from there. Of course, my goal with anyone I work with is to spend the least amount of money possible to yield maximum results. Even when working with high-level clients like Katie Couric, I spend as little as possible. David Oh adds that generally marketers should at least try for 100 percent ROI if they're only talking revenue cost and revenue stemming from advertising cost (but give yourself a reasonable time frame to earn it back).

If you're looking to get a million followers in less than thirty days, the amount you'll spend depends on different variables, including what market you're going after and what part of the world you're looking to reach. If you're building a global company or a global brand, the cost efficiencies to drive audiences in emerging markets are cheaper. In the United States or the United Kingdom, I've been able to generate followers for as low as six or seven cents. In emerging markets like India, with average to good content, you can often get a follower for a penny or even less.

We will cover this topic in depth in chapter seven, "Go Global," but now I'd like to address those of you who are skeptical about the benefit of building fans in emerging markets or have heard people say, "Fans from India are fake." Fans from foreign countries are real people. India, for example, has the second-largest population in the world with 1.3 billion real, live humans. Some of the smartest investors in the world and companies like IKEA, Netflix, MTV, the Coca-Cola Company, and PepsiCo are investing heavily in the Indian market. Facebook just announced that their largest user base is India, with 251 million users, and they have also focused on growth in countries like Malaysia, Turkey, and Saudi Arabia. When the biggest investors in the world are paying attention to foreign markets, you'd be a fool to write them off.

You also have to consider the quality of your content. The better the content, the better the ROI. If you have great content and can benefit from a global audience, you can gain one million followers in less than a month (even as quickly as a week if you do it right) for as low as $7,500 to $8,000. You could also take a hybrid approach—use the strategies from this chapter to generate 250,000 to 500,000 followers quickly and then leverage the information later in the book, such as on forming strategic alliances in chapter six—to generate the remaining followers organically.

In any case, some financial investment is required. It may sound like a lot of money, but if I came to you and said, "Your dream will be more accessible for $7,500," is that worth it? How much is a movie deal, model contract, or record deal worth to you? Think about what you can invest, where you're trying to go, and what you need—maybe you don't even need the full one million followers to build more credibility. Maybe you want five hundred thousand or only one hundred thousand followers. Whatever your goal is, this system can surely help you get there.

Erick Brownstein, president and chief strategy officer at Shareability, a company that has created some of the most shareable content of all time, agrees that, regardless of how good your content is, it's essential to amplify it with paid media. Brownstein says that hope is a bad strategy. No matter how shareable a piece of content is, you have to use paid push. There's just too much noise and clutter out there. You have to boost your posts and pay to ignite it. Brownstein's team operates on the claim that "efficient paid is the new organic." Using paid media really well is key. You'll go far if you're smart and get your fans for a fraction of the cost that others spend.

Driving Down the Cost of Acquisition of a Follower

Anyone can use the page like ads on the Facebook advertising platform, but the real game is driving down the cost of acquisition of a follower to as little as possible. To do so, you need to find the right content that matches the audience you want to reach and that gets them to click the Like or Share button. You need to spark motivation or intrigue them by finding content that resonates.

There's a misconception that when you use the ad platform you're just buying likes of followers, but this isn't true. You're paying

Facebook for the opportunity to put a piece of content in front of someone. Then that person has to opt in and like that content, which you can't force them to do. It's like paying for advertising space in a newspaper or magazine. You can pay for the ad, but it doesn't mean that people will call or come in to your business.

When you have great content, Facebook's algorithms pick up the fact that people are resonating with your piece of creative, which allows you to spend less. Facebook's advertising system operates as an auction. If your content is really good and people are responding, Facebook will keep running the ad and let you run it for cheaper in the auction. On the other hand, if you have a poorly performing piece of content, Facebook will allow you to keep running the ad, but your cost will be extremely high because the content isn't as valuable to the platform. This is Facebook's way of policing the system and making sure there's valuable content in the ecosystem.

Whether people like, comment, or share your posts it gives them more exposure and allows you to spend less to market your content. This concept isn't anything revolutionary and can be likened to processes that took place off-line before the digital age.

When the Beatles first started, they were playing at venues throughout the United Kingdom and Europe. They often had to pay to go to those venues, and in the beginning they funded their own tours. If they hadn't played well or people didn't like their music, they wouldn't have had a good return on their investment. But since they did do a good job (or a great job by most music-loving people's standards), their success spread. They got more and more fans because they were valuable and word of mouth spread the message about their music. The same concept applies to digital—if your content isn't good, it won't spread. And if it is, it will—provided people have the opportunity to respond to it.

So how do you know if your content is good enough and resonating? Look at the metrics. If people share and like your content, you're in a good position. And always keep our friend ROI in the back of your mind. If it isn't happy, you need to pivot. Take the data from the advertising platform and leverage it to understand what it will take to get people to follow you. What content are people sharing? Are people clicking through to your blog? What does it take to get someone to buy a ticket or make a transaction of any kind? Discover the system that works best for you.

Practical Applications

I'll walk you through how to target your audience, choose a message, fine-tune your message through testing, and create shareable content over the course of the next several chapters, but first I want to give you some practical tips for how to implement your ads on Facebook, since these ads are the key to driving people to your page.

Stick with the Facebook Bid Amount

Facebook's ad platform suggests the amount you should spend on your ads. Depending on the ad unit, it's usually anywhere from eleven to twenty-five dollars. I typically stick with that bid amount. I don't fluctuate from it, and if I do, I always spend less. *I never spend more than the suggested amount.* The more you increase your daily bid, the higher your cost will be in the auction.

A common mistake I see people make when running ads is increasing the bid amount in the middle of a campaign. Perhaps they start with an ad that runs for twenty-five dollars a day and performs well. The person gets excited because they see that it's working, so they want to fuel it; they move the bid from twenty-five to one hundred or five hundred dollars. The problem is, when one does this, Facebook resets the cost in the auction. Perhaps they were getting a penny per page like, but when they raise their ad spend from twenty-five to one hundred dollars, it resets and costs will increase and be inflated.

Here's what I recommend: When an ad set is working really well, duplicate it and create a new one. Create an additional ad at the original twenty-five dollar amount and find a new piece of creative or another interest level to help the ad reach more people. Changing these variables allows you to create new variations.

Separate Each Interest Level

It's really important to separate each "interest" when creating the ad. Don't create one ad lumping all interests together. For example, if you're a motivational speaker, don't put "happiness," "depression," "self-help," "motivation," "inspiring," and the like in the same ad set. Create a separate ad for each of those interests. You should do this for two reasons: First, lumping all the interests together doesn't allow you to learn. If all the interests are listed in the same ad, you won't know which specific interest is driving the performance. Second, separating interests allows you to maximize the reach of the creative. If you have ten interests and they're all lumped into one, you can't create multiple duplicates of the ad. However, if you take the same piece of creative and build a separate ad for each of those ten interests, you'll have ten ads that are running at $25, for a total of $250. Doing this allows you to further scale your ads.

What Kind of Content?

When I built my followers I used a lot of pictures with quotes because it's a fast and effective way to create content. It's easy to find and create quotes that match your brand or message. Videos are much harder to create at a high quality, but if you can create high-quality videos, they do perform better.

To figure out which images and quotes work best, you need to go in and test every imaginable variable. Take an image and test five different quotes against it. You can also take a single quote and test five different images against the quote.

You have to find the best way to express your message so it's not a passive experience for your audience. Create content that people look at and say, "I like that. I'm going to share it," or "I'm going to click this Follow button because I like what this brand represents." There will be more on mastering content creation in chapter five.

The Power of Targeting and Dark Posts

Before we cover targeting in more depth in the next chapter, you're going to need to understand an important aspect of the Facebook ad platform. When you run an ad on Facebook, it's considered a "dark post"—a news feed–style ad that doesn't publish to your Timeline or your follower's feeds organically.

A dark post is seen by the audience you select in the ad platform, which is based on the gender, interests, age, and other attributes that you select. This is good because it allows you to test content without bombarding your audience. That way you get to learn what works without annoying your fans. You wouldn't want to push fifty different variations of the same creative to your main feed because it would look like you're spamming the system.

However, dark posts don't automatically exclude all your followers. Here's an example that demonstrates what I mean. I recently completed a test for Under Armour's (a company that manufactures footwear as well as sports and casual apparel) UCLA sponsorship. We tested social creative for this sponsorship by targeting fans of "SportsCenter," "Fox Sports," "UCLA," and "UCLA football." If someone followed Under Armour and also followed SportsCenter, they may see the dark post ads. If you don't want this to happen, you have the option of excluding followers of Under Amour or whatever brand account you're running the ad from.

Facebook gives you the control, and that's the power of the platform. Many people just boost posts to their own followers. But doing this doesn't teach you anything. Use Facebook as a market research tool. That's where you can gain a lot of value and learn what it takes to get people to follow you and engage with you.

I also recommend targeting the broadest age and country range possible so that you can allow the Facebook platform to guide you. You can look at the metrics and see which audience is yielding the best results. Then, in subsequent tests, you can hone in more specifically on what you see working. Start broad and then get narrower.

Launch at Midnight

I usually launch my ads at midnight because that gives the content a fresh twenty-four hours to be tested. Sometimes the auctions are buggy and launching ads later in the day makes Facebook try to fulfill the inventory too quickly, which won't give you the most economical cost in the auction. So create the ad whenever you want but schedule it to run at midnight.

You may be thinking, "What about my audience? Aren't they asleep then?" The fact is, there are more than two billion people on the Facebook platform, so someone is always awake and using Facebook. If on the off chance no one views your ad, Facebook simply won't serve your content until people actually sign on. You won't be charged anything until someone views your ads.

By launching at midnight, you're immediately running the ad for seven or eight hours, depending on how much you sleep. I am not a night owl, so I personally check my results in the morning, but if you stay up, you could check within the first few hours and start optimizing campaigns. It's up to you—it's absolutely not necessary to stay up late at night or sacrifice your sleep to have success.

I've never seen an ad increase performance—regardless of whether I'm using page like, video views, or website traffic objectives—by more than 30 percent after an hour. That means that if you're at fifty cents per like, you're not going to drop down all of a sudden to a penny or even ten cents. You could drop from fifty cents to thirty cents, and that could be worth it. In my experience, if the creative isn't resonating with the audience right away, it's not going to happen. My advice would be to turn that ad off and move forward with another. That said, I have heard e-commerce experts say when they use the cost-per-lead (CPL), cost-per-acquisition (CPA), and load-to-value (LTV) objectives, they've seen success with letting an ad run for a few days. You'll never know what works best until you try it, so test everything yourself and see where you're finding the best results.

Analyzing the Metrics

When I run page like ads my rule is domestic should cost no more than ten cents per page like (the lowest I have generated is five cents) and worldwide no more than a penny per page like (the lowest I have generated is $0.004). But that's my personal standard and the level of performance I'm trying to achieve. I recommend setting your own threshold. Some people may not get that performance based upon their quality of content, and other people may do better. Test and see what works.

If you're using the strategy of making content go viral, my rule is that if your cost per share (CPS) is at fifty cents per share, you're doing OK—anything above that is a sign your content isn't resonating with your core audiences. Anywhere below a CPS of thirty cents means you've got great content, and a CPS of ten cents is rock star status. You can find your CPS by customizing your view in Facebook Ads Manager.

> ► For more info on the basics of the Facebook Ads Manager, please visit www.optin.tv/fbtutorials.

Always see how far you can push your performance. One mistake I often see people making is that they think, "Oh, it's giving me thirty cents per share. I guess that's what I have to pay for it." Instead of settling for that price, try to drive down the cost and increase the performance as much as possible. Don't get lazy; push the envelope.

Test and Learn

We'll be covering the importance of this more in depth in chapter four, but the most vital aspect of this system is *learning*. You've got to understand why something works versus why it didn't. Otherwise, you're not getting smarter. If you don't think about it, then you could end up testing thousands of variations and not generating the performance you want. Don't waste your time. Analyze the data and learn. All this testing and learning is extremely valuable to developing your short- and long-term content strategy, which will drive organic growth.

If you do so, you'll surely be rewarded. Once you start to leverage intelligence from testing, your real growth with people who share your content becomes exponential. Magician and social media entrepreneur Julius Dein, who generated more than fifteen million followers in fifteen months, is a testament to this fact. He says,

> You got to work up the ladder. It takes you some time to hit step two and step three, but then it multiplies fast. When I hit a million likes, I was like, "Bloody hell, that took me so long to get to a million." Then I hit two million in a matter of weeks. And it was the same process on Instagram. I hit my first million only two months ago, and now I'm already almost at three. I bet you getting to four, five, and six million will be even faster.

Building your following takes time, effort, and money, but think of those ROIs. Think about the validation and credibility that will be coming your way. Have this in mind with each creation and ad-set duplication—you'll be one step closer to expanding your audience and reaching your dreams.

Quick Tips and Recap

- Content is the most critical factor when it comes to growing and engaging large audiences online.
- The key to scaling a massive audience in the shortest possible time is an agile approach of producing, testing, and measuring how people are responding to your content in real time.
- Hypothesize, test, learn, and pivot.
- You don't have to reinvent the wheel; look around and borrow ideas from what works for other people.
- Facebook is the easiest platform to gain one million fans on because it's centered on the concept of sharing.
- There are two ways you can use the Facebook ad platform to generate a following: (1) Make a piece of content go viral to gain mass awareness or (2) use a page likes ad unit to target people to follow your page.
- Building an audience requires an investment in either time or money.
- This system does not allow you to buy followers. It allows you to pay Facebook for the opportunity to put a piece of content in front of people.
- To drive down costs, stick with Facebook's suggested bid amount. Only spend more by duplicating the ad with a different interest or piece of creative.
- Always think about your ROI and work backward. If an ad isn't meeting your goals, turn it off.

CHAPTER 2

TARGET YOUR AUDIENCE

T argeting can make or break a business. Many products and brands are capable of reaching a large audience, but knowing the nuances about who will actually engage with your product or brand is what truly helps create a significant lasting following and customer base. As we discussed, in order to scale quickly you will need to find the people who'll not only share your messages for you but also buy your products. As we will discuss later in this chapter, there are different targeting strategies and techniques for specific goals. Furthermore, reaching the right audience will save you time, money, and energy.

Let's say you're selling women's yoga pants. It wouldn't make sense to target men since they aren't the ones who will need or use the product (unless you're targeting them around a specific holiday and promote the pants as a gift idea). Or maybe you're selling Philadelphia Eagles Super Bowl T-shirts—you wouldn't want to target fans of the New England Patriots right after they lost in the 2018 Super Bowl, right? It would be a waste of your resources. Or imagine that you live in a town where everyone is vegan. You wouldn't open a steak house there. Your business wouldn't survive.

Targeting the right people allows your business to thrive. And if you know exactly who your target audience is, the internet—social media in particular—has made it easier than ever before to listen to consumer feedback. Clothing companies like Zara completely rely on their buyers' suggestions for tweaking their designs—corporate headquarters reads thousands of comments from shoppers and uses that feedback to create the next clothing line. It's a user-generated approach to fast fashion, which they claim is one of their keys to success.[1] This is also part of the reason that Zara dominates the fashion market—it's hard for other brands to keep up with that level of attention to the target market's feedback.

Get Specific

We live in the information age, which makes granular targeting more important than ever before. There's a lot of competition—with a myriad of products, messages, and content, people have an incredible number of options. Consumers and fans have become much more specific in their interests, and there's a plethora of niche audiences. Use this fact to your advantage.

If you could take a time machine to the 1970s and stop ten people on the street to ask them their top ten favorite songs, most of

---

[1] Derek Thompson, "Zara's Big Idea: What the World's Top Fashion Retailer Tells Us About Innovation," *Atlantic*, November 13, 2012, https://www.theatlantic .com/business/archive/2012/11/zaras-big-idea-what-the-worlds-top-fashion -retailer-tells-us-about-innovation/265126.

those people would share around five or six of the same songs. People had limited choice of music back then because there was less music being produced and fewer distribution outlets for that music (i.e., only radio and TV).

If you were to conduct the same survey today, there's no way you'd have as much overlap. There are more songs available, more music distribution outlets, including self-distribution platforms (e.g., Facebook, iTunes, and Spotify), and more direct access to the artists themselves than ever before. The level of content, information, and products in the marketplace has significantly increased, fragmenting people's interests into specific niche areas.

This truth applies to many industries. Just look at what's happened to television since the creation of streaming services like Netflix, Amazon Prime, and Hulu. There are more options and styles of shows than ever before. There's an audience for almost any genre—you just need to know how to find it.

With Facebook and other online advertising tools, you can target very specific audiences for your brand. For example, you can target college graduates that make $75,000 a year, who live in Chicago, Illinois, who are married and love dogs. Before the internet, it was much harder (if not impossible) to reach a vast number of people in such a specific group. Using Facebook's targeting features creates an opportunity to figure out exactly who will buy your product and to design your content and strategy specifically to meet their needs, which in turn allows you to be more cost efficient and increase your profitability.

I personally benefited from Facebook's ad platform by using it to target audiences to help me choose the title and the cover of this book. My team tested the creative artwork against different audiences that taught us not just which book cover (down to the specific color) works best but also with which audiences it most resonates. We tested the cover of this book against "entrepreneurs," "small business owners," "people that read publications such as TechCrunch, *Wired*, and *Fast Company*." This information helped us understand who would be most interested in the book and which marketing messages are most appealing to them.

A Targeting Checklist

This is a very broad checklist that will not necessarily cover all your specific targeting goals, but it will help you begin to break down your target audience if you are starting from scratch. To reach the right people, you need to have a picture of them in mind.

Begin by writing down all the information you know about your product or brand. Think about whom it is most accessible or useful to. Once you've compiled a list or a few paragraphs, ask yourself the following questions:

1. What is the **GENDER** of your target audience? Are you targeting men, women, or both?
2. What is the **AGE** of your target audience? Are you targeting younger teenagers, adults, people in their thirties, or another age bracket?
3. What is your **DESIRED MARKETING GOAL**? What is the action that you want your audience to take? Are you trying to

   a. increase awareness about your brand;
   b. sell a specific product;
   c. get people to register for your email list;

    d.   get more engagement on posts;

    e.   drive traffic to a blog or website; or

    f.   do you have a different marketing objective?

4. Where is your audience **LOCATED**? Are you targeting people all over the world, just in the United States, or another country? Perhaps you have a local business and want to target a specific zip code, town, or state? The location of your audience depends heavily on your marketing goals and what you're trying to achieve. You need to know if you're selling a product directly to people in a specific region or if you're trying to build brand awareness and credibility? However, if you work in entertainment or are trying to build a global brand, being known throughout the world can be very beneficial. (More on this idea in chapter seven, "Go Global (an Opportunity)," to help you understand how targeting a global audience could be beneficial for increasing your brand's validation and credibility.)

5. What **INTERESTS** do people who buy your product or brand have?

    a.   What type of music do they listen to?

    b.   What sports do they play?

    c.   What fashion brands do they wear?

    d.   What stores do they shop in?

    e.   What is their routine on a typical day?

    f.   What events do they go to?

    g.   What are their values?

    h.   What kinds of hobbies do they have?

    i.   What are the names of the products that they use?

    j.   What type of cars do they drive?

    k. What television shows do they watch?

    l. What are their favorite movies?

    m. Which celebrities do they follow?

    n. What other interests do you think they may have?

6. What is some additional **LIFESTYLE** information you know about your audience?

    a. Are they married, single, or divorced?

    b. What level of education have they completed?

    c. What is their occupation?

    d. What is their yearly income?

    e. What needs do they have?

    f. How does your product or brand make your consumer's life better or easier?

7. Who are your top-level **COMPETITORS** and what do their fans look like in regard to the questions on this list?

Answering these questions will help you understand the people that you target for your initial testing and will ultimately help you to acquire new customers. The more you understand about the type of people you believe will be interested in your product, the better.

When you start testing the variables you defined above, act like a mad scientist. Try as many combinations as possible. Segment out different variables into separate tests. If you were selling women's yoga pants, your trials might look something like this:

- Test 1: Age eighteen to thirty-five that likes Lululemon
- Test 2: Age thirty-six to fifty that likes Lululemon
- Test 3: Age eighteen to thirty-five that likes Lululemon + is a college graduate

- Test 4: Age thirty-six to fifty that likes Lululemon + is a college graduate
- Test 5: Age eighteen to fifty that likes yoga
- Test 6: Age eighteen to fifty that likes meditation
- Test 7: Age eighteen to fifty that likes yoga + lives in Chicago
- Test 8: Age eighteen to fifty that likes meditation + lives in Chicago

The above is just one example, but you can see that the number of tests can scale very quickly. Always try to test as many variables as possible, until you find the answer you are looking for. Always keep testing to improve your results.

> ▶ To learn more about how to build out these test campaigns, visit www.optin.tv/fbtutorials.

You also need to check that your assumptions are right. To help make sure you're on track if you don't already have an existing fan base, David Oh of FabFitFun suggests getting off-line and talking to your hypothetical target audience. If you think your consumer base consists of women between eighteen and thirty years old, go out and speak to people in that demographic. See how they feel about your message, ideas, and content. Use your friends, family, and acquaintances as resources to help you do market research.

If you already have an existing fan base with people who engage with your content and buy your products or services, there are additional ways to conduct market research. You can mine the analytics from your social platforms (like Facebook Insights) or use information gathered from Google Analytics to learn about who's trafficking your website. You can also analyze prior purchase orders and conduct

surveys with your existing fan base and customers. Use any analytics or data about your audience to help you determine who will most resonate with your content, products, and brand.

David Oh, for example, uses data analytics from his website to better understand the core demographic of the buyers of FabFit-Fun's subscription boxes. This information provides him with their age, gender, beauty/fashion product interests, and the names of the brands they like. Oh even surveys customers on which aspects of the products his customers liked in previous boxes and what products they would like to see in the future. He then leverages that information to create more effective marketing campaigns, which have allowed his company to scale.

Another example of applying these tactics comes from the movie industry. When a movie is made, a rough cut of the film is tested in market research screenings. The purpose of these test screenings is to get the ideal target audience into a theater to screen the movie before its release. Producers and studios bring their intended audiences into the theater, have them watch the film, and then give them scorecards to record their observations, feelings, and opinions about the movie. The movie producers and marketers then use that information to truly understand the people with whom the movie resonates. The data from these test screenings is then used to direct the marketing strategy/positioning as well as to improve the film.

A Market Research Case Study:
Florence Foster Jenkins

Once, my team and I did a market research test for Paramount Pictures on the 2016 movie *Florence Foster Jenkins* with Meryl Streep and Hugh Grant. Paramount wanted to test how to position the movie to their target audiences.

If you haven't seen it, Streep plays the titular character who wants to become a professional opera singer before she passes away. Paramount was struggling to find a tagline for the film. They considered five options, including "You're never too old," "Dream big," and "Every voice matters." But they needed data and analysis to help make the best decision about the core message to use for the film's marketing.

My team tested variations of the taglines against 561,756 people—53 percent female and 47 percent male—in the United States whose interests include "musical film," "biographical film," and "Meryl Streep" since they were most likely to view the film. Reaching an audience of this size with traditional market research, or running these tests on TV, could take weeks and significant budgets. Instead, we completed our tests within forty-eight hours and for a fraction of the cost because we leveraged the Facebook ad platform as a market research tool to segment all these tests and collect data in real time. Once the tests were completed, we quickly compiled the data in an extensive forty-one-page report to make sure we were as thorough as possible with the findings—that way Paramount could make the most informed decision for their campaign.

When we delivered the final report, the Paramount executives were a bit shocked by the level of detail we generated in such a short period. They began to realize they had a new, cost-efficient, and fast data source to help make future decisions about which messages to put millions of dollars behind. And this was all made possible because of testing and conducting our own makeshift market research with the correct target audiences.

A Different Approach to Targeting: Reach Those Who Share

As we have discussed in this chapter, targeting the exact demographic is a great strategy when the sole focus is getting the members to perform a specific call to action (CTA)—for example, click, buy, register. But there is another targeting strategy I like to use that is all about finding the advocates that will share your content and brand

for you. If you're selling women's shoes and need to target eighteen- to thirty-five-year-old women with the CTA of purchasing a specific shoe, then your targeting is straightforward. However, if you can produce great content, then choose the second option. That will get people to share your message at a high velocity, allowing you to generate earned lift from your content and thus drive down the costs of key performance indicators. To achieve this, you should test targeting your messages not only to those who will purchase your product or like your brand but also to the people who are most likely to share your content (which—surprise, surprise—isn't always your target market).

If you're thinking that this targeting strategy is almost the complete opposite of what we just outlined in the earlier part of this chapter—yes, it is. There are multiple effective approaches and strategies, some of which may seem conflicting. But the truth is, what works for one person or brand may not work for another. My aim is to provide you with the most effective options out there so you can test and choose which one works best for you and your goals.

If you're struggling with generating highly shareable content, you may want to begin by using the first approach and getting specific with your targeting. If you are able to create highly shareable content, try expanding your reach beyond the obvious target market and see what the response is. Sometimes the people you want to reach are best attained through others. You may have message champions who aren't in your specific target market but who can reach your target market for you.

Chatbooks Case Study

A great example of finding message champions outside the core target market is a project I worked on with Chatbooks, the number one online

photo printer in the world, with more than a million subscribers. Chatbooks came to me with a Mother's Day awareness campaign in the form of an emotional video about mothers from the perspective of young children. In the video, kids aged four to eight talk about how their mothers are superheroes. It's an amazing piece of creative that was produced by Nate Morley, whom you'll be hearing from later in this book.

Chatbooks told me that they wanted to "target moms aged forty-five and above." After seeing how great the creative was, I knew there was strong potential of people sharing it at high velocity, so I urged them to allow me to test the content and find brand advocates for this video. When I began testing, I used a broad demographic spectrum but was specific in terms of interests related to their product (e.g., scrapbooking, photography, motherhood, and parenting). On awareness and engagement campaigns, I tend to start by targeting the message to reach both men and women, aged eighteen to sixty-five years old (unless we are selling a gender-specific product as mentioned in the beginning of the chapter) and see where Facebook's algorithms push the content within the first few hours of the campaign. I find this to be beneficial because Facebook's algorithms are constantly evolving to help you discover your most engaged audience and will give you useful insights. If the insights are showing that your content is not resonating with a specific demographic or interest level, launch another test. And then another. Keep launching until you find the answers you're looking for. I also suggest you keep a wide target audience on broad-base awareness campaigns because it generally brings down your cost in the auction, giving you more impressions and chances to engage your audience.

While running the tests, I noticed that the people who were sharing the video were actually women between eighteen and twenty-five years old. It wasn't that they were necessarily the ones who would be buying the final product, but they were the ones who were connecting with the content. After further analysis, I found that they were sharing the video with their mothers, tagging them in it, and starting a dialogue with their moms about the content.

Broadening the scope to reach the younger women allowed Chatbooks to hit their core demographic in a far more powerful way. They were targeting the emotional connection between mothers and daughters. In turn, this also allowed them to expose the product to a new audience.

That's where I see the power of shareability and using a broader approach to targeting. It can increase awareness of your messages and content, help you find brand advocates, and, most important, reach your core audience

in an influential way—by getting a friend to share with another friend or loved one. Essentially, you hack word-of-mouth sharing, which is one of the most difficult things to achieve in marketing.

Get creative and allow yourself to make connections between your buyers and your message sharers. You may discover new ways to market your product or brand as well as gain new fans, boost your social numbers, and sell more stuff.

Don't Make Assumptions

Latham Arneson, former VP of digital marketing for Paramount Pictures, adds that many people assume that they know whom to target. Although a lot of the time they're right, plenty of times they're wrong. He explains that with movie marketing you start with a pretty broad set of parameters—for example, "young females." The truth is, that's a large group and there's going to be a lot of different interests within it. Finding out who in the demographic is most willing to share is an important point of focus.

Although centered around marketing films, Latham's experience and expertise can apply to people who are establishing a brand or trying to generate growth. When a movie is not part of a well-known series or franchise, movie marketers are given the nearly impossible task of creating a brand within a six-month period, which is what many of you reading this book are trying to do.

Latham notes that testing is key. He feels that you make some good guesses, but you actually figure it out by testing. That's when you really learn who's interested based on the reaction to the content you're creating. At the end of the day, you can't be 100 percent certain until you actually put it out in the world and see who responds.

When you're dealing specifically with video views, Arneson suggests looking at the video completion rate or the video view-through rate, and then also the correlative action after someone has viewed a video. It's great if a viewer watches 75 to 100 percent of the video, but it's even better if they're watching a significant percentage and then taking a specific action, like sharing that piece of content. Use the people who take leading actions, like a share or a click (on a video, image, or link), as the best indicators of your target audience.

Targeting Campaign Objectives

A part of targeting is choosing the type of ad that will reach your campaign objectives. You can target the ad to gain video views, website traffic, lead generation, post engagement, event responses, and the like. In my experience, I have found that each objective gets weighed differently in Facebook's auction.

Let's say you have a video you want to promote, but you choose the lead generation objective. Your cost per view is going to be inflated because Facebook won't look at it from a cost-per-view perspective. It'll try to drive as many leads as possible. So on any video ad, whether it's to build lead generation or traffic, I typically recommend starting with the video view objective. Doing so allows you to drive down the cost per view to as low as possible to reach the largest audience. Reaching more people means gaining more opportunities to get others to share your message for you. More sharing means more earned lift, which brings down your overall cost per lead. And, of course, this is also obviously great for those who want to generate brand awareness and large numbers. However, if people are not sharing, you may be best suited with a lead generation or conversion if you're just interested in selling a direct product.

If I were to create a hierarchy, post engagement or video views would be at the top of the list, if you have good content. If you have average to below-average content with the main objective of just trying to sell a product, then use lead generation or the website conversions objective. Test and learn—as I've mentioned, it's the only way you'll figure out what works best for your brand.

Retargeting and Look-Alike Audiences

After some testing and learning you'll know the demographic and interests of your core audience and you'll start to observe the type of people who are most likely to share your message. Once you've collected that data you'll want to be sure to retarget the people who *engage* with your brand.

Erick Brownstein of Shareability explains that his team always retargets to get new content in front of those who engaged with the first set of content. He points out that if a person was willing to engage once, they're very likely to engage again. His team tests "a gazillion different target groups" and then, based on the audience that converts or takes the desired action, starts building look-alike audiences and tests those as well.

Tim Greenberg, chief community officer at the World Surf League, also agrees that it's smart to find look-alike audiences. First, he figures out who visits the company's website by using Facebook Pixel, an analytics tool that helps you measure the effectiveness of your advertising, to track website visitors (you can also use Pixel to examine the actions people take on your website and better understand how to reach your intended audience[2]). Next, Greenberg checks to see who's registered for the World Surf League mailing list. Then he analyzes the people who've visited the World Surf League platform and those who've watched their live stream—these are the core users, the core fans who take the initiative to come and watch their content. Greenberg's team simply needs to alert these people with an awareness message that the content is there.

When this process is complete, they focus on the second ring of viewers—they extend out to *look-alike audiences that mirror the original fans*. This audience comprises people who have similar-looking demographics, interests, and additional parameters. They may not yet be fans of surfing, and may not have visited the website, but perhaps will be inclined to do so. His team groups these people into a different targeting bucket and sends them a similar campaign that's adjacent to their core campaign.

Greenberg's team has discovered that the further they go out from the core and core-plus audiences (the audience that has similar interests and characteristics to, but is not part of, the core audience), the less likely people are to convert into watching a surf contest, even if they've liked a piece of content. So his team tries to be really careful. They've discovered that hitting audiences that either look like or are their core consumers are the best people to target. Having more likes may look good, but when it comes to actually converting

---

[2] "The Facebook Pixel," Facebook Business, https://www.facebook.com/business/help/651294705016616.

to some form of action it's important to stick to the audience discovered through the data.

The Facebook platform has brought the World Surf League a lot of new fans. Because of Facebook's scale, the league has amassed an audience they wouldn't have been likely to reach otherwise. It's allowed them to capture data and test their product and content on new audiences—to drive new fans to their owned and operated sites. Greenberg's team has built an engine to capture new fans and retarget them with either a merchandise message, a tune-in message, or a download-app message. It's been really beneficial for their company.

Fun Fact: Hypertargeting Can Trick Rocket Scientists

If you get really smart about targeting, you can reach just about anyone on Facebook. FabFitFun's David Oh once told me a story about a trick he played on people at the Jet Propulsion Laboratory (JPL), a federally funded research and development center and NASA field center in La Cañada Flintridge and Pasadena, California. Oh went there to give a lecture about using Facebook's digital marketing and hypertargeting—the act of sending highly targeted messages to very specific groups of people. If it sounds familiar, it's the type of targeting discussed earlier in the chapter, that zeroes in on demographics like age, sex, location, language, education, interests, and workplace.

Before going to the lecture, Oh did a little experiment. He made some fake ads on Facebook and used them to target anyone who worked at JPL within a twenty-mile radius. One ad was for something called "Life on Mars?" The ad had a rover with a question mark on it. Another ad said, "Funding for Next Rover Project Canceled?"

He made ten different variations of fake ads with various headlines and images. He had also heard from a friend that there was an inside joke at JPL that people were called "peanuts," so he made a landing page, which people were redirected to when they clicked on the ad, that said "Peanut Community News" with a little countdown timer set to when he was giving his speech.

Oh spent about two dollars on that effort, and he had about ten clicks. Four scientists even put their personal emails into the email waiting list he created. During the lecture, he explained what he did (blurring out names so he wouldn't embarrass anyone), but two of the IT people at JPL stood up and said, "It better not be any of you."

The point is, the hypertargeted ability of Facebook's ad platform makes it possible to trick rocket scientists. So if you know your audience, it allows you to do very well on Facebook or any other place that offers this kind of granularity.

Quick Tips and Recap

- There are two strategies for targeting:

    1. Targeting the exact demographic is a great strategy when the sole focus is to get them to perform a specific CTA (e.g., click, buy, register).
    2. If you're able to generate highly shareable content, you can leverage a strategy of testing to identify advocates who will share your content and brand for you.

- If you're struggling to create highly shareable content and are focused on direct-response marketing campaigns (i.e., selling a specific product or service), taking a narrow approach with the targeting checklist is the best place to start. Paint a picture of your audience by exploring aspects of their personae, including gender, age, what action you want them to take, location, interests, and lifestyle.

- If you're running broad-base campaigns and trying to drive mass awareness, start broad with your targeting and see where Facebook's algorithms push it. Keeping your target audience wide generally brings down your cost in the auction.

- Use Google Analytics and social media data such as Facebook Insights to help you mine data about your target audience.

- Analyze prior purchase orders and conduct surveys with your existing fan base to help you determine with whom your content, products, and brand most resonate.

- The campaign objectives' priority is post engagement or video views if you have good content, and a conversions ad if you're just trying to sell a product and have average to below-average content.

- Test a gazillion different target groups.

- Don't assume you know who your audience is; allow new target groups to be discovered.

- Retarget your content to whoever engaged with the original content.

- Build look-alike audiences of the people who converted or took desired actions like sharing or clicking.

- You can't be 100 percent certain who your audience is until you've actually put your content out in the world and seen who responds.

CHAPTER 3

CHOOSE A MESSAGE FOR THE MASSES

O nce you have built up your followers and understand who your primary audience is, you need to keep them engaged. You must create content that keeps your followers wanting more, that resonates with their interests, and that gets them to share your brand at the highest possible velocity. This is the best way to make sure your message continues to appear in your audience's social feeds. There's no point in building up followers if you can't have active engagement. Creating content that grabs people's attention and makes them want to share it with their social friends and connections is key.

Knowing how to structure your message is critical to success. If what you're saying isn't capturing your audience's attention and causing them to engage with your content, the work you put in to build that audience goes to waste. Getting fans isn't enough. You need to continually captivate them; it's important for the continuing growth of your audience and social followers.

Although I can't give you the specific messages that will be best for your brand, since everyone's will be different depending on goals and target markets, I can give you guidelines that will help you discover how to choose the best messages for yourself. By following these simple guidelines, you will know how to stand out among the noise in no time.

Find Your Hook Point

To share compelling information, you have to find a unique hook point—that is, something that makes you stand out, grabs your audience's attention, and leaves them wanting more. It's an essential exercise in understanding the value of what you have to offer.

A great example of a solid hook point is what Tim Ferriss did with his book title *The 4-Hour Workweek*. Ferriss had a concept and an idea of the type of value he could offer the world, but he needed a hook to get people to pay attention to his message and stand out. If he hadn't found a succinct, thought-provoking message, his book wouldn't have been a bestseller. The novelty of a four-hour workweek was what grabbed people's attention. The concepts in the book were nothing revolutionary or new, but Ferriss's ability to package these ideas with the concept of only having to work four hours a week was something that sparked people's interest. It was a tangible lifestyle image that people desired and didn't know how to get. It hooked them into wanting to know more about this enticing and interesting offer. If Ferriss had used the title *The Tim Ferriss Guide to Working*

Fewer Hours, it wouldn't have been as captivating. Instead, he thought about what would resonate with the audience he was trying to attract and how the wording could hook them. He figured out what they wanted and didn't only focus on promoting himself. By coming up with a catchy way to explain this material and through creating an image of a lifestyle choice, he got people's attention.

It's not enough to simply talk about yourself and explain what you do. Many other people have the same skill sets you do. You have to find what makes you and your product or information unique and relevant to other people's lives.

What makes what you do different? And how can you make that important to others? You have to come up with a succinct, attention-grabbing way to get your information across. And it needs to be relevant. You must associate yourself with topics that are timely, interesting, and meet your audience's needs. The hook point is what gets people to stop and pay attention.

Find Your Headline

Here is an exercise I like to use with clients for discovering their hook point: Imagine you're given the cover feature article about you or your business in a major magazine or newspaper publication. Now imagine that a potential customer is walking down the street and passing a magazine stand. What headline would grab their attention and get them to stop, buy the paper or magazine, and read your article? Make sure to put yourself in your customers' shoes. Be really honest about what would get someone to stop what they're doing and pay attention to your message. Remember, there are more than sixty billion messages sent out every day. Your hook point needs to help you STAND OUT.

Headlines are important in all kinds of industries. The 1999 movie *The Blair Witch Project* was a huge success because the marketers behind this movie understood how to choose a headline. They based the campaign around the idea that the story was real, which grabbed people's attention and made them want to learn more. These were the headlines they created: "In October of 1994 three student filmmakers disappeared in the woods near Burkittsville, Maryland, while shooting a documentary . . . A year later their footage was found"; "Everything you've heard is true"; and "The scariest movie of all time is a true story." These headlines (or taglines, as they are called in film lingo) captivated the viewer's imagination and left people curious about what happened. Many wondered if the movie were actually true, which enticed them to go see it. Also, the idea of the filmmakers disappearing moved people on an emotional level by provoking fear and curiosity and made them feel invested in the story.

Another movie that had a good tagline is *Paranormal Activity* (2007): "What happens when you sleep?" This is a concept that grabs people's attention because it's a question that most people are curious about and have asked themselves before. If your headline asks questions that your audiences are already asking themselves then your headline is strong.

Good headlines stand out. An example of a great news headline is "The Truth Hurts: The Million Dollar Video Game Competition." It attracts attention because "The Truth Hurts" is specific, succinct, and evokes an emotional response. And combining it with "The Million Dollar Video Game Competition" perks interest because most people have not heard of a video game competition that offers a million dollars as a prize. This is a headline that could get many people to watch at least five seconds of a video or read a bit more about the article. It's relevant to people's lives and taps into their needs, wants, and desires.

Another strong news headline is "Buckingham Palace: Police Injured Arresting Man with a Sword Near Buckingham Palace." This captures your attention because it's not every day that a man with a sword is attacking people. It's something unique, has a royalty/celebrity angle, taps into people's fear of the unknown, sparks interest, and grabs attention.

Now that you're starting to become familiar with headlines that work, let's look at an example of a headline that's not effective: "Trump Under Fire." This headline is too vague and doesn't really make you want to click on it (unless you are just obsessed with knowing anything associated with President Trump). This could easily be improved by replacing it with one of these headlines: "5 Reasons Why Trump Will Be Impeached in the Next Year," "New Details of Mueller's Investigation Point to Trump's Eventual Impeachment," or "Mueller's Investigation Reveals Shocking Details on Trump's International Business Dealings."

A/B Test Your Headline

Once you are clear about what you want to communicate, you can use A/B testing to find the most effective way to communicate it. Maybe you're at a point where you know what you have to offer, are clear about your value, but still aren't sure about the catchiest way to grab people's attention with your message. That's where my system can really come in handy. You can take your core messages, test them against each other, and in real time determine which one is performing best.

To make sure that your headline is captivating, test different variations against each other on Facebook. You have variation A and variation B. Let's go back to the four-hour workweek example to understand how to use it to test a headline.

Tim Ferriss used Google AdWords to test the title and cover of his book, which was extremely smart and part of the reason that his book became a bestseller.[1] But that was before Facebook developed the sophisticated and detailed targeting options that it has now. If Ferriss used my system today, it would be like what he did back then *on steroids.*

To begin, we would want to choose a target market, such as men between eighteen and twenty-five years old who speak English, live in North America and Europe, and who are interested in entrepreneurship. We would set these parameters with variation A, *The 4-Hour Workweek*, and then duplicate them for variation B: *The Tim Ferriss Guide to Working Fewer Hours.* By testing these two titles against each other in real time, we could gather a lot of interesting information about which message better grabs people's attention.

The Facebook platform is great for these tests because it allows you to get very specific with the data you are testing and with whom you would like to target for the test. You can check how a specific message resonates with different genders, ages, specific interests (e.g., movies, books, art, and cars), types of digital platforms, annual

---

[1] Cory Doctorow, "HOWTO use Google AdWords to Prototype and Test a Book Title," *Boing Boing*, October 25, 2010, https://boingboing.net/2010/10/25/howto-use-google-adw.html.

income, net worth, and purchase behaviors. It allows you to gather very specific data that can be useful for altering your message, campaign, or even the product you're selling.

You'll be certain of whom your message resonates with. And you don't have to spend a lot of money to get great results. With as little as ten dollars you can learn a wealth of valuable information that will help you discover the most effective messaging for your needs.

The Psychology of Communication

Many times the content that you share isn't as important as the context you wrap it in. To get the most out of your content, you need to be a great communicator. Social media was designed as a form of two-way communication. And the goal of communication is always to reach the person you're communicating with. Jeff King, an expert in the Process Communication Model (PCM), a behaviorial observation tool that allows you to communicate more effectively, has been highly influential in the way I, and many major corporations in the world, create content and communicate with others. The PCM was founded by Taibi Kahler in the 1970s and has been used by very successful and influential people ranging from President Bill Clinton to NASA astronaut selection officials to producers at Pixar Animation Studios.

King explains that when he gives seminars on the PCM he always starts off by stating that communication isn't about you (pointing to himself), it's about *you* (pointing to a person in the audience). Communication's true use is getting information to the people you want to reach. And to effectively reach someone, you need to speak a language they understand. The PCM can be extremely helpful because it helps you assess the communication style of the person you're commmunicating with. Doing so allows you to better tailor your message so the person who needs to receive it can hear it easily and clearly. King's experience has shown him that we are often very selfish in the way we communicate; we usually think more about our need to express than the person who is listening on the other end—and this is a mistake. If we want others to hear us clearly (and in turn share our message further), we need to step outside ourselves and truly connect with the other person. The PCM is a tool that helps us do this.

The biggest mistake I see people make, and that I help correct when working with clients, is creating content through the lens of how they perceive the world and failing to recognize that much of the population perceives the world in a different way. Thus, their messages don't get across clearly. When developing content for an audience, make sure you're not just creating it for yourself. You need to look at your content from the perspective of your audience. Spend time thinking about how your audience might perceive that piece of content or message. This is where the PCM comes in handy.

King explains that content has to connect with people before they're going to share it with others. And different people connect in different ways. People who perceive the world through feelings are going to share content that makes them feel good, whereas others may perceive the world through logic and respond well to content that speaks to their reason. Whatever content resonates with them the most will be the content they choose to share.

In the PCM there are six personality types: Thinkers, Persisters, Harmonizers, Imaginers, Rebels, and Promoters. Each personality type experiences the world in different ways. Thinkers perceive the world through thoughts, and *logic* is their currency. Persisters perceive the world through opinions, and *value* is their currency. Harmonizers perceive the world through emotions, and *compassion* is their currency. Imaginers perceive the world through inactions, and *imagination* is their currency. Rebels perceive the world through reactions, and *humor* is their currency. And last, but certainly not least, since they are often very powerful people, Promoters perceive the world through actions, and *charm* is their currency. All the personality types are in each of us, but we have a base personality type that we're born with and that doesn't change over the course of our lives.

Let's try an exercise of creating copy to advertise a car. Using the PCM, King explains how he would construct the content to make sure that he communicated the clearest message about the car, wrapping it in a way that makes sense for each of the personality types. King suggests writing something like this:

> Think of a car. This car model gets fifty miles per gallon. The car's miles per gallon are at the highest rate compared to other models in its class. We believe that this car provides more value to our customer in regard to what you're going to pay for. Bottom line—it's the best car on the market. It feels good, it looks nice, and you're going to be so comfortable driving this car. All your friends are *finally* going to want to hang with you because this car's awesome.

Now let's break this down to which personality type each sentence speaks to:

- This sentence uses **LOGIC** and speaks to Thinkers: "Think of a car. This car model gets fifty miles per gallon. The car's miles per gallon are at the highest rate compared to other models in its class."

- This sentence uses **VALUE** and speaks to Persisters: "We believe that this car provides more value to our customer in regard to what you're going to pay for."
- This sentence uses **CHARM** and speaks to Promoters: "Bottom line—it's the best car on the market."
- This sentence uses **FEELINGS/COMPASSION** and speaks to Harmonizers: "It feels good, it looks nice, and you're going to be so comfortable driving this car."
- This sentence uses **HUMOR** and speaks to Rebels: "All your friends are *finally* going to want to hang with you because this car's awesome."

As you can see, the ad is written to speak to all the personality types (except Imaginers because they're harder to connect with in this context). Thinking this way allows you to reach a very large audience and speak to all kinds of people, and content has to connect with an individual before that person is going to share it with someone else. Those who perceive the world through feelings will share content that makes them feel good. Those who perceive the world through humor will want to make their friends laugh, too. Whatever content speaks to them the most will be the content they choose to share.

If you understand how your audience perceives the world, and you incorporate it into your communication style, it can be very effective in helping you develop content. King shares that to reach the majority of people in the population, it's best to focus on *feelings/compassion*, which speaks to Harmonizers, who make up 30 percent of the North American population; *logic*, which speaks to Thinkers, who make up 25 percent; and *humor*, which speaks to Rebels, who make up 20 percent. King recommends focusing on those three personality types to create content that reaches a very broad audience. That way you'll tailor your content so that most of North America can really hear, understand, and engage with your message.

The PCM has proved so powerful and effective that politicians at the highest level use it. One of the key turning points during the 1996 presidential election was when Bill Clinton won a critical debate against George Bush. King explains that during the debate there was a woman who asked a question about how each party would help people in her situation—her family lived in poverty and struggled to eat. Bush responded to the question with thoughts and logic as well as value and opinions. However, the woman perceived the world through feelings and emotions, thus Bush's answer didn't connect with her. On the other hand, Clinton picked up on her communication style right away, and before answering the question Clinton addressed her by saying, "I feel your pain." He connected with her on a deep level. He saw that she was a feeling-based person (like 30 percent of the North American population). By using those words, he immediately gained the trust of the people in that group and made the woman (and people like her) feel understood and heard.

Clinton is known for having mastered the PCM technique. King shares that it helped him become president of the United States because he focused on including feelings, logic, and humor in his speeches. People may not agree with all of Clinton's ideologies, but most feel that he's a great communicator and that he's speaking directly to them. He studied the technique in depth and knows how to identify a person's personality type very quickly. Also, when he speaks to a broad audience he's sure to hit all the currencies.

Remember, it's not always about the content but rather the context you present the content in. Construct your messages so they connect with all the different ways people perceive the world. Communicate the same message in different styles. This allows you to maximize the reach of your content and, ya know, have more of the attention you crave. (Just kidding. Remember, it's about giving. Please tell me you've been paying some attention.)

Be Relevant

When thinking about how to structure your headline and what message to share, there are some trends you can follow. Your headline will go nowhere if people aren't interested in your content. You must find a way to take what you have to offer and make it accessible by linking it to what is already working. Popular content that gets shared often can be grouped into five categories:

1. Inspirational, motivational, and aspirational
2. Political/news
3. Entertainment
4. Comedic
5. Pets

Whether or not your brand is directly connected to these types of content, you can use them to your advantage. By finding a way to link your message to what is already popular, you can increase your views and shares. You need to analyze your core message, your hook point, and tie in relevant, popular trends to your specific messages.

When I was building my fan base, I tapped heavily into inspirational and aspirational-based content. I linked my message of building followers and using social media more effectively to helping people pursue their dreams. Linking my message to people's dreams enabled me to more effectively grab people's attention than if I had just said, "This is the best way to use social media." Once I generated a million followers, my hook point changed to "Zero to a million followers in thirty days." Using this hook point, I created a video campaign on Facebook that generated more than five thousand applications in sixty days from people all over the world wanting to hire me to learn how to implement my system.

I also used some political-based content in conjunction with a podcast that I did about the PCM. My message is not political, and I'm not involved in politics, but I knew that using a political angle when doing my podcast interview with Jeff King about the PCM would give the content a strong hook point. We could tie this message to the election between Hillary Clinton and Donald Trump, which a lot of people were talking about and felt very passionate about at the time. By connecting the PCM and Jeff King to something relevant and topical in people's lives we made the content more accessible.

It would have been really boring to promote this information by saying, "The Process Communication Model is behavioral psychology that helps people communicate more effectively." It's too vague and no one would pay attention to it. Instead, I took the message and tied it to different pop culture references that would spark people's interest. When I interviewed King, I made sure to also ask him about the personality types of top celebrities and public figures. I used the headline "Discover Why Tom Cruise, Leonardo DiCaprio, and Donald Trump All Have the Same Personality Type." That kind of headline captures your attention much more than just saying that the PCM is a useful communication method.

> ▶ You can see exactly how I tied relevant and topical themes to the PCM by listening to the podcast interview here: www.optin.tv/jeff-king. You can also view the Facebook videos we created from this interview on my page: www.facebook.com/BrendanJamesKane.

You can find popular tie-ins for almost any message, and it's necessary even when your information falls into one of the five categories. I have a friend named Stephanie Barkley who is a comedian and an up-and-coming Instagram influencer. She heavily promoted herself and got out the message about her comedic skills by creating a skit about Melania Trump. Stephanie is still growing her fan base, so she needs to create content that is engaging, entertaining, and captures the attention of people that don't know her work. If she used a headline like "Stephanie Barkley Creates Great Comedic Sketches" the message would be too distant and irrelevant to most people's lives. It would also be ineffective in building up her following and would only be relevant to die-hard fans. But "What Melania Trump Really Thinks About Living with Donald Trump" grabs a broader audience's attention.

I can't stress enough that with sixty billion messages sent out on digital platforms each day you have to stand out. The great news, however, is that of those sixty billion messages, a vast majority aren't relevant or interesting. So this gives you an advantage. Capitalize on this fact and make your information relevant. Create messaging that your audience is interested in.

Make It Emotional

Another question you should always ask yourself when creating content is, "Will this content create an emotional response in the viewer?" Any content that can get an emotional reaction out of those who see it is valuable. When creating a piece of content and thinking about the message, ask yourself if it can get someone to laugh, cry, smile, feel angry, feel motivated, or have a strong opinion about what's being said. Emotional messages and content get people to share. If the content moves your audience internally, there's a greater chance that they will make an external move to share it with others.

Also linked to this idea is the concept of social currency. Jonah Berger's 2013 book *Contagious* explains the psychology of what affects our behavior, illustrates how to get people to share messages, and introduces the idea of social currency. Social currency is content that we share because we feel that it reflects well upon us to share it. We think sharing it makes us look smarter and as though we are being helpful to others.

BuzzFeed has had tremendous success deploying the social currency tactic on the Facebook page for their food brand Tasty. In September 2017 Tasty's main Facebook page was the third-largest video account on Facebook with nearly 1.7 billion video views. Tasty creates simple instructional how-to recipe videos that teach people how to make delicious food in a visual format. By sharing these videos fans feel that they are helping their friends learn how to make dishes that will bring joy to their family and friends. And it makes them feel important for sharing information about a topic that's valuable to many people (almost everyone loves great food). People share this content at a high velocity because it gives them social currency.

The sharing of articles surrounding actor Bill Paxton's death also illustrates the effectiveness of this tactic. The articles about his death evoked a strong emotional response and people were sharing the information. Some people were sharing it because it was emotional, while others were sharing it because it gave them social currency—they felt valuable for being the first person to tell the world that Bill Paxton died.

For some reason, celebrity deaths are a topic that, when used appropriately, can be very helpful with your messaging strategies. One time, I created a website with resource information to help treat drug and alcohol abuse. This isn't a very sexy topic. People are often embarrassed and don't want to be associated with addiction. It's content that's usually difficult to get people to like or share. But I figured out a way to make it more accessible and shareable for the public.

By tying celebrities dying as a result of drug and alcohol abuse, and talking about celebrities that are struggling with addiction, I made this important and helpful information more shareable. I linked the resource information to rock star Chris Cornell's death and also to stories about certain Kardashians struggling with drug and alcohol abuse.

I played into this celebrity angle to draw attention and get people to come to the website. They may have gone there to read this high-level celebrity gossip, but the article had substance to it. It had information about what to do if you or someone you know is struggling with addiction. People were coming to the content for entertainment—and I'm sure there's a big percentage that didn't see the value beyond that point—but there was a decent subset of people who took away some helpful advice about drug and alcohol abuse. The information weaved in made them think twice, and perhaps they then had resources to help a family member, friend, or even themselves if they were struggling with those issues.

Again, there's plenty of information out there about drug and alcohol abuse. It's not a new topic, but creating a messaging strategy that helps the information stand out and gives it a unique hook point that grabs people's attention is key. The message becomes more relevant to more people.

> ▶ You can look at Facebook to find out which topics are trending and learn from those messages. The trending topics can help you choose which content to share on a specific day and can show you examples of headlines that are generating interest. This information can help play into new story angles and link your content to topics that are already generating interest.

Katie Couric Case Study

Katie Couric once came to me with a problem. At the time, her very successful career had been built on a TV-first distribution model. She had broken the barrier by becoming the first woman to solo host the evening news and had twenty-plus years of television experience on prominent shows like *The Today Show*, *NBC Nightly News*, *CBS Evening News*, and ABC News, which made her one of the most important journalists in the United States. Katie was reaching millions of people every day, and her fans were trained to tune in at the exact same time to consume her content. They knew that every morning they could see Katie as they prepared for their own day. Katie was part of their routine.

Then, in 2013, Katie made a drastic change by forming a partnership with Yahoo! Although Katie was a digital pioneer and had embraced social media from the time she worked at *The Today Show*, she still found herself thrust into a digital-first strategy, which completely changed the habitual relationship with her fans. Because of this, fans were constantly telling her that they were having trouble finding her content. There was no longer a specific time her content could be consumed, and her fans were struggling to find and establish a relationship with Katie.

In our very first meeting, Katie asked me what could be done to solve this issue. She needed a quick solution. I asked her when her next interview was, to which she responded, "Two hours from now." I replied, "Perfect! Plenty of time to come up with a new strategy." She was going to be interviewing actress Elizabeth Banks. I took a few minutes and explained that we needed to identify topics that would evoke a strong emotional response in specific audiences and that would result in them sharing her content with their peers at a high velocity.

Elizabeth Banks is an actress in the *Hunger Games* and *Pitch Perfect* series and is also an outspoken feminist leader, so these were the specific topics we structured the interview around. We crafted questions that had the best chance of evoking a strong emotional response from fans interested in those topics. From there, we cut multiple thirty- to ninety-second clips from each of these interview segments and created fifty to one hundred variations of each clip. Then we A/B tested them against each other on Facebook to see which variation and audience was sharing the clip with their peers at the highest velocity. We created specific content around *Hunger Games* that we pushed to *Hunger Games* fans. We also created specific content for *Pitch Perfect* fans and for feminist supporters. Doing this made non-Katie Couric fans interested enough that they were willing to share Katie's brand. Then, once we had that level of shareability, we were able to say, "Hey, listen, if you like this clip of Elizabeth Banks talking about *Hunger Games*, why don't you come over here to Yahoo! to watch the entire interview?" The strategy was to use die-hard fans around specific topical matters, celebrities, and news stories to share the content for Katie to not only reach Katie's core fan base, but also to expose new audiences to her content. Breaking it down that way generated mass exposure for Katie *and* for the Yahoo! brand.

Over the course of sixteen months, this formula was used for all Katie's interviews. It generated over 150 million views, increased social shares by 200 percent, and saved Yahoo! tens of millions of dollars in traffic acquisition costs. Her typical TV interview reached a few hundred thousand viewers, and with this new strategy we were now averaging well over a million views per interview. Our top interview was with Brandon Stanton, the founder of the photoblog *Humans of New York*. This interview alone generated more than thirty million views and was shared over 300,000 times. Additional successful interviews featured prominent celebrities and public figures such as DJ Khaled, Joe Biden, Gal Gadot, Bryan Cranston, Deepak Chopra, Chance the Rapper, Edward Snowden, Skrillex, and Jessica Chastain.

We sent millions of people every month to Yahoo! to watch Katie's interviews. People were coming up to Katie on the street and telling her they were seeing her content again.

Why did this process work? Over the course of sixteen months, we ran more than sixty thousand content variations across two hundred interview segments. I regularly told Katie not to fall in love with any specific segment. Instead, if an interview didn't perform, we looked at the data, identified why it didn't work, and improved it for the next one. With this agile messaging approach, we learned very quickly what was working and not working in regard to syndicating Katie's content and brand at the highest level. With each interview we were learning and building Katie's content and messaging strategy. We got to a place where we could identify exactly whom to interview, what topics and themes to cover, and even specific questions to ask. Ultimately, our content strategy allowed us to quickly adapt Katie's content from the habitual TV-first consumption behavior to a digital-first consumption behavior, all by figuring out which messages mattered.

Now it's your turn. Take that information and apply it to the next piece of content you create. Find the ways to link your messages with what's already popular to get people interested in what you're doing.

Quick Tips and Recap

- Define your hook point by knowing what makes you unique.

- Choose a great headline by making it specific and relevant.

- Adapt your content to what your audience is already interested in.

- A/B test your headlines against each other to discover which is the most relevant and useful.

- Use psychology and human behavior to communicate your message clearly to different types of audiences. Speaking in a way your audience can understand is key. Remember, according to the PCM, focusing on **LOGIC, HUMOR, AND EMOTIONS** will resonate with the majority of the North American population.

- Find messages that make your audience ask themselves questions they're already thinking about but don't know the answers to.

- Determine whether inspirational, political, comedic, entertainment, pet-based, and social currency can be leveraged to attract attention to your content.

- Create content and messages that move people emotionally.

- Know which topics are trending on Facebook and online.

CHAPTER 4

FINE-TUNE THROUGH SOCIAL TESTING

We've already discussed and driven home the importance of testing in relation to my system. This chapter is a continuation of its importance and the strategies and philosophies that some of the top digital minds use to approach testing. To discover what will work for your audience you must allow yourself space to test, play, and discover. If your content doesn't resonate, keep testing and tweaking until you find the content that does. As Katie Couric says, "One of the most important things I learned from Brendan is to be nimble." If something doesn't work, it's fine; you just need to learn from it and pivot on the spot.

I want you to develop the habit of constantly testing—observing your audience's responses and knowing how they engage with your content in real time. Analyzing the results helps you understand the effectiveness of your content strategies. That way you generate immediate feedback loops. It's one thing to get the analytics and data, and it's quite another to actually learn from them. You need to look clearly and be honest with yourself. If something doesn't work, don't get overwhelmed and frustrated. Look at it and ask yourself, "OK, why didn't this work? Why did this piece of content over here get shared a thousand times while this piece of content only got shared once?" Analyze both spectrums of what did and didn't work. Then you can start making hypotheses about your short- and long-term content strategies. Observe which content encourages someone to engage, to follow your page, to share your content, to buy your product, and the like. Use the Facebook ad platform (that also powers Instagram, WhatsApp, and Facebook Messenger) as a market research tool as we discussed in chapter one to really understand what it takes to get someone to perform a specific action.

The Value of Testing

Testing is not a new concept—everyone from scientists to business owners have used it. Deliberate experimentation was even the key to Thomas Edison's success when he created the lightbulb, and currently it's Facebook's secret weapon. In fact, according to an article on Medium.com, Facebook usually has ten thousand different versions running to test what will be most effective for users. Founder Mark Zuckerberg says that experimentation is the defining strategy of his company's success.[1]

---

[1] Michael Simmons, "Forget Practice—Edison, Zuckerberg, and Bezos All Show the Secret to Success Is Experimentation," *Business Insider*, January 4, 2017, https://flipboard.com/@flipboard/-edison-zuckerberg-and-bezos-follow-the-/f-9637670253%2Fbusinessinsider.com.

The basic principle of testing comes from science where it's laid out as "theory, prediction, experimentation, and observation." In business, the model is broken down as "plan, do, check, act." In my system, it's "hypothesis, test, pivot." Essentially, it's all the same. To create anything, this is the process that works.

David Oh of FabFitFun says that if you want to grow you have to test. He urges companies to implement systems and processes to measure and observe and then act decisively as many times as it takes. His company tests everything on their website and social media platforms, even seemingly trivial considerations like pictures and colors (on ads and landing pages), styles of buttons, catchphrases, and the number of forms for users to fill out.

Think of yourself as a student. Successful people are willing to fail and learn. It's the basic process of life. Although gaining one million followers is an abstract concept, Oh says it isn't much different than learning to walk. When we first learn to walk, we fall down. When we're building one million followers, one hundred million customers, or $100 million in revenue, we also have to keep falling until we learn how to do it. You have to create a regimented process of doing it over and over again. That's what successful people do in all walks of life. They test and learn and use their learning as fuel.

David believes that the process itself is valuable. It's important to be malleable. First you think of something, try it, and then adjust accordingly. You can learn from a mistake, a mild advance, and a great success. Then you create varied versions. You do this process over and over again—it's a type of perseverance that everyone knows intuitively.

Jonathan Skogmo, founder and CEO at Jukin Media, a company that currently gets close to three billion views a month and has more than eighty million followers across all channels and verticals, agrees and says that his team is testing content all the time. They observe what works and what doesn't. They test different content, different thumbnails, and the time of day they post. Testing is a huge part of the culture at Jukin Media.

Tim Greenberg's team at the World Surf League does the same. They put out multiple video assets for all campaigns. Whether they're doing a Billabong Pipe Masters or a Pro Tahiti awareness campaign, they'll put multiple assets in market with different variations on either the copy or the format. Then they test those against the same audience. And ultimately, they run with the ones that are the most successful—the ones that survive the testing phase.

Never Stop Testing

Prince Ea says that you continue to test and learn even after you've created two billion views. The process never stops because you're constantly pushing yourself to try new things.

The most important thing is to actually learn from the results. What I notice is that people often get lazy. They'll test five or ten variations, and unfortunately, 95 percent of the time, those variations aren't going to yield optimum results. They won't resonate with the largest-possible audience. People get frustrated, but they need to keep testing. Most people won't hit it out of the park right away. At first, your cost per follower probably won't come in super low and your content won't go viral—it could, but if it does, it will probably only happen to less than one percent of the people reading this book. Even I rarely do that. I'm constantly testing, learning, and pushing the boundaries of the platform. Besides, the more intelligence you glean from the tests, the better you'll be at producing good content. Take time to learn how to dramatically drop the cost per share or whatever your essential key performance indicator is.

Chris Williams, the founder and CEO of pocket.watch, an entertainment company for kids, and former chief audience officer of Maker Studios, who also launched Disney Online Originals (a division of The Walt Disney Company dedicated to the creation of Disney-branded short-form content), advises that you should look at content the way engineers look at software. Put it up, see what happens, iterate, see what happens, iterate, and see what happens again. The beauty of digital platforms is that you can create content and iterate very quickly, unlike TV or magazine features where that process takes much longer. The beauty of social media is you can immediately see who's doing well and get inspired from what's already working out there. Go out, test content, measure the response, and iterate quickly.

How Many Pieces of Creative to Test a Day?

You should constantly be testing and pushing yourself and your brand, but how many pieces of creative to test per day depends on how many interests are related to your brand. How many targeted keywords/interests can you find to represent the audience you're trying to build? If you only have ten interests that are relevant to your brand, you'll need more pieces of creative. If your brand has a broader scope, you could potentially have two hundred ad sets (to learn how to set this up, visit www.optin.tv/fbtutorials).

If you're an actor, for example, you could target not only those interested in directing or producing but also people who like every single film that resonates with their brand—and there are hundreds of potentially relevant films. On the other hand, if your brand is related to sports, perhaps there are only twenty relevant interest levels that could be turned into ad sets. It all depends on the subject matter.

Using quotes and matching them with photographs is an easy-to-follow model that I highly recommend starting out with. Once, I built a million followers in two weeks for a nonprofit dedicated to protecting the ocean. We targeted about twenty different interests. The creative was a quote matched with an image of the ocean. I used ten images and ten quotes. Each image was matched with one of the quotes and then each of those variations was tested with between ten and twenty interests. We tested about a thousand variations of content. The three most successful variations were:

1. A quote by marine wildlife conservation and environmental activist Paul Watson that said, "The oceans are the last free place on the planet," with a photo of a woman paddleboarding next to a beautiful wave;

2. A quote by oceanographer Sylvia Earle that said, "No water, no life. No blue, no green," accompanied by a video of one of my friends paddleboarding next to a gray whale mother and her young calf;

3. A headline that said, "One of the many beautiful reasons to protect our oceans," with a photo of a whale's tail sticking out of the water before it dives deep into the ocean.

Testing one thousand variations allows you to learn. You will find that even one little tweak to a word or to a background color can make all the difference in the world. And although it may sound

tedious, by duplicating the ad sets you can create a thousand variations in under an hour. Build one ad set and then keep duplicating
and swapping out different interests. You don't have to build the
quotes from scratch—just duplicate by changing out slight variables.

To decide which ads to leave running, think about your goals. If
your goal is a penny per follower and all the ads are generating that
result, you leave them on. You always turn back to the equation "I
want to hit a million followers and I want to do it for ten grand." If
this is your goal, then you need to hit a penny per follower. If the ad
is not yielding a penny per follower, you simply turn it off and try a
new variation that gets the results you're trying to achieve. Remember to test and measure at scale as many types of content as possible
to learn what best resonates with your audience.

When I spent the month building a million followers, I would
measure—in real time—the response rate of which content got
people to follow me. I would test hundreds—and in some cases,
thousands—of variations to determine what yielded the best results.
Every night at midnight I would launch between a hundred to three
hundred variations of content, and when I woke up in the morning I
would measure the results and set a new test for the next night. Over
the course of thirty days, I tested more than five thousand variations
of content.

Listen to Your Audience

One of Hollywood's most successful movie producers, media executives, and investors, Jon Jashni believes in listening to your consumer. He highlights that you should view them *as your partner* in
this process. If you're constantly pushing bite-sized offerings of your
artistry to them, you create a connection. They can receive what you

offer and give you immediate feedback. They can literally tell you that they loved the content you posted.

It's valuable to receive this feedback from your social media network in ways that are understandable and actionable. And be quick to respond to them because if you take them for granted they'll go find another platform that seems to care more.

Search Tools Help You Listen, Test, and Learn

Latham Arneson, former VP of digital marketing for Paramount Pictures, shares that Google AdWords can be leveraged as a tool to clarify what people are already searching for. It helps you understand the keywords that you're targeting. This is not the same thing as putting content in front of people through social platforms. The big difference between social and search methods is that social is a push model, while search is a pull model. Seeing content in the Facebook news feed is more comparable to TV advertising than it is to searching on Google for something specific. People can still comment on content in Facebook, but it's not the same as going to Google and seeking out information—that shows a much more active level of interest.

Search-based tools allow you to test messaging and observe how people are talking about different topics. You can see if there's search activity on keywords related to your brand or product—if people are actively wanting to discover more. Search gives you a good indication of how your message may perform.

When Arneson's team worked on the 2008 movie *Cloverfield*, for example, they noticed that people searched for terms related to the film, such as "JJ Abrams," the producer of the movie, and the film's release date (they initially used the release date as part of a marketing hook because they had not yet announced the name of the film). When they observed the keywords that were searched for most often it created a feedback loop letting them know which aspects of the marketing materials made the most sense to push in future campaigns.

AdWords can also help you compare how searchable your content is against other similar brands and products. Arneson adds that there's a public tool called Google Trends, which gives you a relative search level so you can see if you're looked for as often as other brands. These tools are extremely powerful. They give you insight into competitors' situations that you can't get anywhere else. If people are searching for you more often than your competitors, it's a strong indication that your product or brand will sell.

Some of you may not be at the level where people are searching for your name or product, but these tools can still be used for content intelligence. Arneson says that if, for example, you're launching a yoga brand, you can see what people are searching for in regard to yoga and use that to direct your content marketing decisions. You can find out if people are more interested in yoga mats or towels, or if there are any jokes or new topics related to the yoga world. Knowing this information can help you determine where to focus your efforts. It can even help you in making business decisions. You will learn what's hot and which products to push.

Additionally, these tools can help you determine your market size. You can get a sense of interest level before you develop a product or piece of content. Facebook can also give you a sense of interest by telling you that ten million people "like" yoga, but a search-based tool shows you how many people are actually searching for a specific product or term. The fact that people are seeking it out makes it more active and pragmatic.

Social Listening

Social listening is the process of monitoring digital conversations to help you understand what customers are saying about a particular brand, person, or industry online. It's used to surface feedback that can help differentiate your brand, product, or service. Arneson's team at Paramount used social listening to understand which aspects of films people most connected with. His team would observe the films that did really well and pay attention to what people were talking about. Was it the story that captured their attention or the characters? This is valuable information that helped them understand how to market current and future films. It helped them learn what people were excited about.

It's important to know that this process takes time and a lot of data analysis. Arneson urges that you can't just look at the top queue of subjects that people are mentioning. You have to dig deeper and find out why they're talking about what they're talking about. You have to interpret the messages and use your best judgment to create new content or adjust the content you have and see how people respond. Then you listen and adjust accordingly again. It's an ongoing observation-and-testing process because it's never clear-cut. People won't come out and say, "I love this video because it makes me feel really good about myself." It will never be that obvious.

Arneson advises that it's important to watch trends change over time. Observe how people respond to your content or product at the onset, and then notice how their reactions change as time goes on. Doing so gives you a backstory to understanding what type of content and messages are important to push. Over time, you'll develop the ability to use what people are saying to inform your ongoing efforts and change the conversation to meet their needs.

Having the backstory will also give you a grounded point of analysis to help determine if there are comments you can ignore. Perhaps a person complains about a piece of content. But then you go back and see that in the past others enjoyed similar posts. If you have the data, you'll have a point of comparison to keep things in perspective and determine which problems, if any, are worth reacting to. If you've kept records over time you'll have a broader picture and clearer understanding of how and why people are engaging with you.

If you're a large brand and the amount of information is overwhelming, you can always hire a company to help you perform social listening. However, most of you are probably at a stage that's manageable enough to do it yourself. Just read and record the comments on your posts and use the search tools that social platforms provide to look up keywords around your content. Additionally, you can go to your competitors' pages and record the comments and information about the type of content that's performing well and not performing well on their social pages. Make sure you record what you learn so you can go back each week or month and do a comparative analysis.

Ask Your Consumers Questions and Think from Their Point of View

Arneson adds that it's important to create clear distinctions between what you're testing. Don't simply change a word—that's not different enough. Test fundamentally different messages. That way you'll have a good understanding of what people prefer. Ask your consumer questions by giving them different messages to choose from. If you put four clearly distinct messages out there, and your audience overwhelmingly gravitates toward one of them, you'll have no doubt about what they're interested in.

This is a different approach than what I use since Arneson comes from the movie industry, where testing different messages is critical to understanding how to tap into a specific audience. I agree with what he's saying, but I also like to tweak different words to see if some slight variation can dramatically increase performance in some way. It doesn't always work, but sometimes it can take you by surprise.

Try to think from your consumers' point of view. What is your audience going to experience when they see your content? What, if anything, do they already know about your brand? If they've experienced anything about your brand in the past, do you think they'll remember it? Understand who the consumers are and where they're at in terms of knowledge of your content and brand.

Another reason it's important to test and listen to your specific consumers is to find your most original and compelling voice. Often, we think that a content strategy we've seen work for other brands will automatically work for our brand as well. But this isn't always the case. Just because other brands and people are using a specific format to market a product or content doesn't necessarily mean it's the best way to approach marketing *your* brand or *your* message.

Dollar Shave Club is a perfect example of a brand that found an original way to market its content. Before it came along, shaving razors were mostly sold through TV spots, and Gillette was the predominant player. Then Dollar Shave Club came out with a funny, crazy, tongue-in-cheek online video that represented its new brand[2]

---

[2] "DollarShaveClub.com—Our Blades Are F***ing Great," YouTube video, 1:33, posted by Dollar Shave Club, March 6, 2012, https://www.youtube.com/watch?v=ZUG9qYTJMsI.

and gained more than four million views. At the time, Dollar Shave Club was a young start-up, and it was hard to compete with Gillette, but by understanding social media, listening to its audience, approaching things differently, and testing they were able to break into a highly competitive industry.[3]

With this campaign, Dollar Shave Club started a trend, and since then people have copied it again and again. But it doesn't always give its competitors the results they desire. Each brand needs to figure out its own identity and what its specific audience is interested in. And you need to do that too.

Leverage Your Community to Fuel Decisions

Ray Chan, CEO and cofounder of 9GAG, an online platform for humor, has built a company with 39 million page likes on Facebook, 44.5 million followers on Instagram, and 15 million followers on Twitter. Globally, it's one of the largest media entertainment brands and one of the top thirty most followed pages on Instagram. Also, if you take away celebrities from that list, it's ranked number six.

Ray uses feedback from his community to vet which content has the most viral and highest-quality potential. The feedback his brand receives by observing its audience's responses allows him to make decisions about what will be posted on its social channels. If something's going to perform well, it usually happens pretty quickly.

---

[3] David Vinjamuri, "Big Brands Should Fear The 'Dollar Shave Club' Effect," *Forbes*, April 12, 2012, https://www.forbes.com/sites/davidvinjamuri/2012/04/12/could-your-brand-be-dollar-shave-d/#7e3f32b94854.

The team tests a lot of content within the community and lets the successes drive future posts.

9GAG's content is fun and humorous in general, which makes it accessible to a lot of people. His team is based in Hong Kong, but 9GAG's user base is very international. Its followers are not only from Hong Kong but also from the United States, Germany, the Netherlands, Indonesia, the Philippines, and other parts of the world. If he relied only on people from his team to design rich content, it would probably be biased. Instead of only having his editorial team decide what works, the brand lets its community—comprising millions of people—become an extended version of the editorial team.

It's really important to keep learning and seeing where the market's going. Listen to your community and let it guide you on where your company and your brand should be focused. Ray also has an app and points out that there's a big gap between what the mainstream media is talking about and what users are doing. For example, if you look at TechCrunch, you would think that tons of apps are very popular because they're featured in their articles. However, most of his users are from a younger demographic and don't even read TechCrunch, so this type of secondhand research doesn't serve his company. He suggests relying on firsthand research by talking to your users directly to know what they like and what they're doing. He is constantly listening to his community and audience to continually learn and improve his overall content strategy.

Take Your Time

Jonathan Skogmo of Jukin Media also believes in testing constantly. He admits that his company's content doesn't magically go viral—it's continuously testing and leveraging data and analytics to get better at choosing the most successful content.

Jukin Media has four different brands that leverage Facebook, YouTube, and Instagram, and they realize each platform has a different audience. Skogmo's team customizes the content to each platform. The same video may have a different length, title, or starting point when posted on Facebook as opposed to when it's posted on YouTube or Instagram. Each platform will have a slightly different version of the content.

Skogmo urges you to take your time in listening, testing, and discovering. The process is not a race but a marathon. "Just because you're not on a rocket ship doesn't mean you're not growing," he says. And if for a moment you are on a rocket ship, don't think it will last forever; at some point you'll run out of fuel.

Get content out there, test, learn from it, and repeat. At the end of the day, you're in it for the long haul. Don't play the short game; go for the long game. Observe your audience's behavior and never stop putting content in front of their eyes.

Quick Tips and Recap

- Test and learn. Then use that learning as fuel.
- Testing is used in all aspects of creation—from medicine to business to science. It's the foundation for learning.
- It's one thing to record analytics and data and quite another to actually *learn* from them. Observe how and why people engage with your content.
- The more intelligence you glean from your tests, the better you'll be at producing content that resonates with people.

This will help you dramatically drop costs around your key performance indicators.

- Ask your consumers questions by giving them clear, distinct messages from which to choose.
- Think from your consumer's point of view.
- Don't get complacent. Push the boundaries of the platforms.
- Listen to your community and let them help you decide which content will be most effective.
- Google Trends and AdWords help you tailor your content to what your audience is most interested in and allows you to observe trends over time.
- Practice social listening by looking at your community's comments on your posts and content. Also, go to your competitors' pages and observe how their content is performing.
- Tailor and test content individually for each platform.
- The testing process is a marathon, not a race.

CHAPTER 5

CREATE SHAREABLE CONTENT ON FACEBOOK

A s you have probably gathered by now, shareability is the most important metric when looking to grow quickly on Facebook. It assures you that your content is resonating with your audience. Getting people to share is also the best way to organically spread your message and stand out from the noise. Having a range of quality content regularly shared keeps you thriving and increases your chances of going viral.

To create a massive following and a steady sense of growth, focus on creating shareable content. You can't push random content to people and hope to keep their attention for long. The best way to keep them coming back for more is to have a strategy that engages and involves your followers. That's how you can scale fast, especially on Facebook.

Sharing Is the Key to the Kingdom

Getting someone to like or view a piece of content is easy, but at the end of the day it doesn't really mean anything. It's a great vanity metric, but it doesn't help you produce results. Someone who shares your content is taking an action. This is feedback that your content is resonating. As Latham Arneson puts it, "Taking action is essential. At some point, you need your audience and consumers to do something, whether it's engage, or buy a product." Having followers sit back and passively like your page doesn't do you any good.

Major social media influencers understand the importance of getting people to share content and this is where they focus their attention. Magician and social media entrepreneur Julius Dein, who generated more than fifteen million followers in fifteen months, explains that his main goal is to get as many people to share his content as possible. "When I'm looking at the videos I share," he says, "I'm not looking at how many views I get. I don't care if the video's got two million views on Facebook. I care about how many shares it has, 'cause if it's got a lot of shares, that means it's exponential."

When people share your content, they're helping you grow your brand. They're actively spreading your message and giving you a more powerful voice. Tim Greenberg of the World Surf League points out that a share on Facebook is the greatest indicator of a successful post. A share endorses content as one's own and proves that people champion and believe in the message.

Greenberg also highlights that getting people to share your posts drives that content to more viewers on the Facebook platform. Facebook algorithms are designed to display highly shared content in more people's feeds. Overall post performance is highly correlated to how often it's shared. Facebook rewards sharing and it's absolutely in your best interest to capitalize on this. As Jon Jashni explains,

> If what your audience experiences is deemed exceptional, worthy, and replicable, they'll leverage their social media networks and become your ambassador, your proselytizers. And they're coming from a generation where the warrant is not easily granted. People are not shy to indict, reject, and attack.
>
> If everyone has been raised to believe that their own personal brand is as relevant as the brands of those who are more widely celebrated, or are more famous, there's an inherent ego in that as well. In that, "If I tell you to go to this restaurant, or watch that movie, or watch that series, or eat that dish—and I'm telling you it's good—I'm the maven. I'm betting my reputation on my recommendation."

When your audience deems your content worthy, they become a powerful force in spreading your message. Also, people are inherently more willing to take a recommendation from a friend, from someone they trust, than from anyone else. People receive content more willingly when they don't feel like they're being sold something.

Sharing Leads to Sales and Direct Actions

The irony is that the less you try to sell the more you will sell. When you focus on creating *value* for people instead of gaining customers, it drives sales and direct actions. Erick Brownstein of Shareability agrees that creating content that's share-worthy is essential. Shareability's team are masters at generating shareable content. Their top twenty videos of 2017 generated 10.5 million shares compared to the top 200 campaigns on AdAge's viral video leaderboards, which only generated 6.4 million shares on Facebook and YouTube in aggregate! And AdAge includes the best videos from Apple, Google, Facebook, Samsung, Budweiser, and more than a hundred other brands. Overall, Shareability has generated more than 3.5 billion views and forty million shares for the world's largest brands.

Brownstein's team uses the Ayzenberg's earned media value index[1] to calculate earned media, which means putting a dollar value to likes, comments, shares, and organic views. Brownstein disclosed that according to the Ayzenberg's Q3 2017 earned media value index, the Cricket Wireless campaign, "John Cena Loves the Internet," drove $122 million in earned media value. And the 2017 music video "New Rules" that they created as an award-winning campaign for Hyatt with the artist Dua Lipa had, as of writing this book, a crazy $200+ million earned video value (with tens of millions of organic views still coming in). The Hyatt campaign has generated a massive ROI in terms of earned media, significantly more than a hundred to one. Fundamentally, these incredible results were driven by the creation and distribution of highly shareable content.

The key is giving your audience value without asking for anything in return. Then, once the video has performed well, you can later retarget the people who engaged with your videos and ask them to take a direct action. But first always warm them up with good content that provides value before following up with a traditional advertisement.

---

[1] "The Ayzenberg EMV Index Report," Ayzenberg, http://www.ayzenberg.com/about/ayzenberg-emv-index-report/.

Brownstein's team at Shareability uses a "full-funnel activation" strategy. First, they start with big, viral, shareable content; then they move on to content that causes additional engagement, but still doesn't push a strong call to action; and last, they push content to people that engaged with the first two pieces of content, asking them to take an action related to their clients' goals.

On the Cricket Wireless campaign, they started with "The Unexpected John Cena Prank" video back in 2015, where John Cena surprises fans who think they are auditioning to be in a Cricket Wireless commercial. When they go to introduce John Cena, he actually burst through a poster of himself. The fans' reactions are priceless—you can see them here: http://bit.ly/UnexpectedCena-Shareability. Shareability launched this video twice on Facebook and generated more than eighty million views overall. In 2017 they produced a second, follow-up video, "John Cena Reacts," which was part of a bigger campaign that Shareability launched called "John Cena Loves the Internet." "John Cena Reacts" was the reverse of the original "Unexpected John Cena." In the second video, fans surprised John instead of John surprising the fans. John was opening fan mail thanking him for his "never-give-up" motto that helped them bounce back from injuries and heartache. Then, as the video progresses, John gets emotional watching a clip of a young boy thanking him for helping his mother battle cancer. After the clip finishes, the son surprises Cena by coming through the same poster from the first video with his mother to thank John in person. John gets extremely emotional and we see a beautiful exchange of gratitude between all involved.

One of the reasons these campaigns were highly successful was because they didn't ask for anything—their only purpose was to provide value to the audience, from making them laugh in the first

Cena video to touching their hearts in the second. The second video became the most shared ad in the world in 2017 and was number three on YouTube's trending videos. On Facebook it drove more than 2.5 million shares and 110 million views on the original upload and more than 160 million total views, including audience reuploads. The entire "John Cena Loves the Internet" campaign gained well over two million total shares across platforms.

After the success of the first two videos, Shareability's team continued to bring value to the campaign by creating ads to retarget the people who had engaged with the content. They followed up with messages like, "Hey everybody, it's John Cena here. Why don't you go to the store and buy that phone?" These viewers typically already feel a strong connection to John (and by extension Cricket) because the original content was emotional and engaging. Fans are more likely to take action when they feel an authentic connection.

Be Service Oriented

From the experience of creating and maintaining one million fans, and through conversations with the greatest marketing minds and social influencers, I've learned, without a doubt, that the best way to get content to go viral is by providing service and value to others. You can't think about what you want or need from people, you must think about what you can offer them. Always start by asking yourself how you can touch your audience on an emotional level that inspires them, that makes them feels connected, or moves them in some way.

One of the greatest Facebook content geniuses today is Prince Ea. He approaches content creation with service as the top priority of his strategy. He admits that even though his ego can (and often does) get involved with the desire for millions of views, he always tries to pivot back to the main goal, which is reaching the heart of his viewers. He focuses on making a true impact on the people who will see his posts and believes that things really take off if he doesn't focus on creating content for his own personal gain. The numbers soar when he figures out how to serve others. He starts to see exponential growth in his videos. Changing his mind-set from a me-focused approach to a them-focused approach transformed his video views from around ten million over an eight-year period to close to two billion views in just two years. Switching to providing value and having a service-oriented approach made him a view-gaining magnet.

Prince Ea believes that although the headline of a video, the thumbnail, the length, and the first few seconds are key areas to have a logical and practical focus, it won't go as far if the content isn't good and doesn't serve others or touch them emotionally. When creating content Prince Ea starts with these questions to put himself in a service-oriented state of mind:

- Why am I here?
- How can I provide service and value to others?
- If this were the last video I was ever going to make, what would it say?
- If this is going to be the best video on this topic, how can I make it the best video ever? What will present the content in the best way it's ever been presented before?
- Why do I share the content that I share?
- What do I like about the content I see?
- How can I have a meaningful impact on the world?

Reflect on these questions for yourself and your brand. If you start your content creation with these questions, you will be able to redirect your focus from personal gain to serving others, which in turn will inspire your viewers to share the love.

Katie Couric takes a similar approach when creating content. She focuses on building a sense of community by finding topics that affect viewers on a visceral level and that can improve their lives, which is why she has done bold and brave things like getting a colonoscopy on national television. After that show aired, the number of people screened for colon cancer went up by 20 percent. It took courage and humility to put herself in a vulnerable position that inspired others to do the same and take care of themselves. This kind of content has an impact on people's lives and makes them want to share the information with others.

Erick Brownstein also takes a service-oriented approach when designing content. He explains that people don't like being annoyed with typical advertisements and marketers must think about and commit to creating value for potential customers. Shareability knows that advertising will only become shareable by creating emotional connections, eliciting strong relational bonds with viewers, and building new relationships. "When people share they care," Brownstein said, "and when they care they buy."

Connect with Your Audience

When looking for content creators who know how to move an audience, I couldn't help but think of Pedro D. Flores, filmmaker and CEO/creative director at Comp-A Productions, a production studio that specializes in social media marketing. He created a video called "Tacos" that has had more than a hundred million views. Flores attributes the success of that video to its relatability. It's a comical video about how he gets discriminated against because he looks white but is actually Mexican. It takes a serious subject and educates the viewer, yet does so in a lighthearted manner. It makes the viewer feel, think, and laugh.

Flores created "Tacos" as a comment on real experiences he was having in his life. He has a very Mexican name, but people always accuse him of lying about the fact that he's Mexican. To combat the frustration, he presented this video in a straightforward way, with no gimmicks, so people could get a taste of what it's really like to be a white-looking Mexican.

When creating content, it's always smart to find things that are going on in your own life that you imagine others might experience. Vulnerability and honesty allow viewers to feel closer to the subject and to connect with you and your emotion. It makes the material more relatable and therefore more relevant to others' lives.

Couric adds that now more than ever it's important that people feel connected to the material:

> I think the ultimate irony in this age of connection is that we're more disconnected in many ways. Loneliness is one of the number one epidemics in the country. Another prevalent epidemic is anxiety, which I think is being contributed to by information overload. It's really important to find the sweet spot of providing a genuine emotional connection with the material.

If you give some thought to the content you share, you have an opportunity to enhance people's lives and make them happier, brighter, and more informed. It goes back to what Prince Ea said about service. Think about how your content can help other people (and, yes, this will also help you get your content shared).

Brownstein suggests asking yourself, "Why should anyone give a damn about my message?" We must remember that there's so much content out there—it's endless. So when you create content, you've got to figure out what will make people care. You have to make them want to learn more and then maybe they will share it with their friends.

Brownstein adds that after you figure out why people would care about your message you need to be sure to deliver the message authentically. Social media is all about building relationships. So when creating content, it's important to ask yourself what having a good relationship with someone looks like. It isn't about simply asking them for stuff. You need to be interested in them. Brownstein offers the idea of looking at the relationship through the lens of a value exchange. Give your fans value and then also an opportunity to offer value to their friends. If you give them funny content to share, they get to feel like comedians; or if you provide them with emotional content, they have the opportunity to touch someone's heart. Other people feel like they're offering value when they educate others on important topics, or they feel like part of a community when they have strong opinions about an issue or a person.

He drives home that relationships are about giving, not just about receiving. Make sure that you're trying to give your audience something valuable. You should follow an 80/20 rule: give 80 percent of the time and ask your audience to take action only 20 percent of the time.

For example, when working with Cricket Wireless the briefing Brownstein's team received was to "create videos that give people something to smile about." Cricket literally spends hundreds of thousands of dollars on these campaigns just to make people smile. It was only after they released several videos with this intention in mind did Cricket ask people to take action from these campaigns related to their business goals. This was a very generous (and smart) approach that demonstrates the 80/20 rule and focuses on creating content that services others first. Do this.

Brownstein also believes that almost any topic, even the seemingly mundane or difficult, can go viral; Shareability even created viral content around pediatric cancer and colon cancer. He feels that especially with difficult subjects it's important to tap into people's emotions and connect with them at the heart level. Are you starting to see the pattern here?

Tim Greenberg of the World Surf League agrees and says that his team focuses on improving the viewer's mood: "If I can publish a piece of content on social that makes someone happier for even three or four seconds then I've done my job. I've actually bettered that person's day through great content."

Creating an emotional connection with viewers is an essential element in making your content relevant to your audience. Think about how your content will make viewers feel and they'll be much more likely to share it with others. Always be conscious of your end goal and *why* you share your content.

Mastering Relevance

Finding the most relevant content for your audience must be discovered through testing and trial and error. There's no exact way to know what will be most relevant to everyone's lives, but Brownstein shares that one way the team discovers ideas for what will resonate is by looking at trending topics on the internet and by observing popular internet memes. Then his team aligns those trending messages to the brands for which they're creating content.

A successful case of creating content based on a trending topic is Shareability's video campaign for Pizza Hut and Pepsi called "The Dangers of Selfie Sticks." The video is in the form of a goof public service announcement about the dangers of using selfie sticks. Brownstein's team got the idea because selfie sticks were a trending topic; for example, selfie sticks had just been banned from Disneyland. Pizza Hut was in the process of launching a two-foot-long pizza, so they came up with the concept that you would need a really long selfie stick to take a photo with this new, unusually long pizza. By making that connection and creating a parody of selfies in general, the video was very funny and went viral on YouTube. It became the most shared ad in the world the month it launched partly due to the relevancy of "selfie stick" in video search at the time.

To reach this level of shareability, Brownstein's team goes through a rigorous process of testing. It samples different formats and openings, and collects data from big focus groups, which are most often conducted by running the content on Facebook and seeing which versions generate the best response (basically, my system in a nutshell).

They analyze each aspect of the content to ensure that it will resonate with the viewer. For example, when they cast videos they carefully select people who are relatable. When creating the Dua Lipa music video that they did for Hyatt, they made sure that the girls were not all supermodels. "If you watch the 'New Rules' music video you'll see that the girls are attractive, but not super glammy," Brownstein explained. "They are more like Dua's relatable girlfriends." Shareability takes this level of care and consideration in each and every decision related to the content. Even seemingly insignificant details make a huge impact.

Don't just take a shot in the dark when trying to create shareable content. Do due diligence and research trends, pay attention to what's working, reverse engineer what other successful content creators are doing, and then put together some low-cost proof of concepts to test. Tests help you become certain about what works before you invest heavily in a single direction for a piece of content. And if you don't have the time, my team can definitely help you in this process.

When in Doubt, Go with Your Gut

Even though I'm a huge advocate of testing and learning (as you may have gathered by now), there are times when you have to let go, let experience guide you, and listen to your inner voice. Trust yourself (which is not the same thing as taking a shot in the dark) because intuition, which is based on life experience, can guide you and help you determine which content will be more or less effective.

Mike Jurkovac, Emmy Award–winning director/producer at TheBridge.co, shared a story about important information he learned working alongside Mike Koelker. Koelker is in the advertising hall of fame for much of his work, especially for campaigns including the Levi Strauss & Co. "501 Blues" for 501 jeans in 1984, and "Colors" for Dockers in 1992.

Jurkovac witnessed Koelker's use of his intuition to give birth to a very special campaign. Jurkovac and Koelker met with the California

Raisin Advisory Board who were trying to figure out how to promote raisins (not the sexiest fruit in the bunch). They were looking at the results from some focus groups and two creative ideas were getting pretty strong results, while the other creative direction wasn't. The farmers couldn't decide which way to go. Since Koelker had built a billion-dollar business, they decided to ask his opinion.

He said, "I know the tests aren't supporting this, but there's just something about those clay-mated characters that I think people will really respond to. Following my gut, I'd go with this." The direction that Koelker chose, the one that wasn't responding well in the tests, became the "California Raisins" commercial of 1986, where the raisins sing and dance to "I Heard It Through the Grapevine"—one of the most iconic and successful commercials of the eighties.

A fun story about Koelker making that choice comes from while Jurkovac was working late on the Levi's account. A man came in and said, "Does somebody here do the raisins?"

"Yeah, that team's downstairs," Jurkovac said. "A guy named Mike Koelker did it."

The person replied, "I had a dream last night, so I flew up to San Francisco because I saw myself as one of the California Raisins. It's not about the money. I just want to be a raisin. The money can go to my charity." The man who spoke those words was Michael Jackson. Michael had seen the campaign and on his own decided, "I want to be that." Jurkovac says that this is the secret to content: make something so great that it *moves* people to take action.

Be Authentic

When developing content, stay authentic to your brand and message. Actor and producer Rob Moran—known for acting in *There's*

Something About Mary; Dumb and Dumber; and *Me, Myself, and Irene*—explains that those movies resonate because their creators didn't grow up in Hollywood, which can often create a barrier to the discovery process. Sometimes when you know too much you become jaded and influenced by what you've seen work or not work. The Farrelly brothers, the creators behind *There's Something About Mary* and *Dumb and Dumber*, were just being themselves and generated content that they thought was funny. They weren't concerned with reaching everyone because they knew their content wouldn't make everyone laugh, but they would make the right people laugh. They didn't need everyone to get their jokes, which gave them freedom.

Today, more than ever, you have the ability to be authentic because digital platforms (especially Facebook) create content distribution that's truly democratic. The content that gets shared is the content that resonates. You either create things that strike a chord or they don't—plain and simple. And these platforms give you the freedom to share things without being at the mercy of a studio's distribution team; you get to do it yourself, which gives you more control.

Play into the Unexpected

We all want to create content that's fun and interesting, and unfortunately there's no set formula or secret to doing it. Your content has to have specific moments that really catch people's attention and you'll have to try out different things until you find a winning combination. However, movie producer Jon Jashni hints at storytelling secrets that may help you get better results. He highlights the idea of playing into the unexpected. Experience has shown him that great movies (which are often storytelling at its finest) are not about shock endings but about outcomes along the way that can't be predicted.

He shares that "unexpected outcomes, unexpectedly timed, makes stories feel fresh."

His involvement with the 2009 movie *The Hangover* taught him that people were surprised because the film was a noir detective story fueled with emotion as much as it was set up with outrageous gags. It was a love story between men, which was original and unexpected. A fresh take was offered on the subject, and it was something people hadn't seen in a while.

Brownstein also notes that the surprise factor has been tremendously valuable in his team's work. The highest-viewed celebrity video of 2015, with more than 180 million views across brand and fan pages, and an additional 520 million views tracked through third-party video ID software, was Shareability's "Cristiano Ronaldo in Disguise—ROC." Cristiano Ronaldo is one of the biggest social influencers in the world and has created hundreds of videos. But Brownstein explains that all prior content had featured Ronaldo in the same light—a *GQ*-style superstar looking amazing with jets and Bentleys. So Shareability decided to give Ronaldo's fans something they hadn't seen before. They dressed him as a shabby busker and stuck him in one of the most popular squares in Madrid. He was playing with a soccer ball, lying on the ground, and attempting to pass the ball and engage with people who, for the most part, ignored him. Then, when a little boy accepts his offer to play, he autographs the soccer ball and takes off his disguise—people's quickly pivoted reactions are priceless. Fans loved the video because it featured Ronaldo in a distinct way and totally surprised them.

Shareability then created a few more videos of Ronaldo displaying him in other unexpected settings. One video showed him playing "Jingle Bells" with ordinary home items (such as a toothbrush) at his house, and another featured him drinking tea at a mall to measure how many sips of tea he could have versus how many people would come by to ask him to take a picture with them. All the videos Shareability created exposed something authentic and different about Ronaldo, something people didn't expect. Shareability actually created Ronaldo's four most successful videos!

It's human nature to want new experiences and to see things in new ways. The Ronaldo videos were successful because they showed an idolized person in an approachable way. Think about how you can surprise your audience and give them the unexpected. Make something that helps your followers feel close to your brand.

Julius Dein adds that it's good to have twists, particularly at the end of a video. He hooks his audience and then tries to have an unexpected ending that creates extreme virality. If people watch the video and think, "Whoa, this is cool. I like this," and then—*bam!*—something ultra-shareable happens at the end, it's a recipe for success.

Expand Your Content Horizons

Tim Greenberg shares findings his team discovered by analyzing the content that performed most optimally over the last year. In 2016 alone, the World Surf League had 1.4 billion Facebook interactions and video views and 124 million total video views on a single post, which was the top video of any sports property last year. Greenberg's team sheds light on why certain pieces of content outperform others. Although you can't predict virality, he says that you can get pretty close. He knows from experience that a video of a drone filming a dog and its owner riding a longboard will do pretty well; it's almost guaranteed to get good engagement. And the highest-viewed piece of content that his team created over the last year, which was actually the number one sports-related piece of content across the board online, was a video of dolphins surfing waves. This success brought up a lot of questions for him about what that means for his business and industry. His company puts on the largest surfing competitions in the world—and naturally talks a lot about surf contests—but it also tries to represent surfing as an aspirational lifestyle and extend the content to people who want to learn how to surf. So he had to ask himself if a video of dolphins surfing is relevant—is it related to the business?

Over time the answer to that question has become yes. The success of the video gave his team permission to have a wider conversation with fans. Surfing is about more than the very narrow spectrum of the competitive sport. It means a lot of different things to a lot of different people. And because it takes place in the ocean, a piece of content related to that visceral experience is valid to people who want to know about and aspire to surf. Ultimately, the content did tie in with the brand's message.

The top ten videos related to sports content in the last year were all of the same nature. The other nine videos were not pictures of the sport itself, but they were related. They consisted of half-time shows, or a behind-the-scenes moment where an athlete gives a hockey puck to a child, or of an anthem being sung by a marine. "It was all the moments that happen next to the event, it wasn't actually the sport that captured people's attention," Greenberg shared.

Examine subjects and moments related to the atmosphere of the world in which your brand exists. What type of content can you promote that creates a heartwarming connection or excites viewers about what you do? Is there a way you can offer them an aspirational or particular lifestyle experience? Perhaps you're unaware of how interesting the small moments in your world are to other people.

Greenberg's team did a Facebook live event of creating the world's first-ever crowdsourced surfboard. They used the live platform to ask fans their requested dimensions for the board and had Hayden Cox build it in real time. This is just one of many fun ideas that the World Surf League has experimented with. Their team is constantly looking to try new things, feature products, broadcast sunsets, and so on—essentially, they don't limit themselves to talking about contests (their product) and look to create a whole lifestyle experience related to the World Surf League. They aim to give fans content that's fun and interesting.

Don't Force People to Share

You may have noticed that a lot of brands get people to share posts by enticing followers to tag their friends or comment on a piece of content. This is an effective strategy, but you need to have a solid reason to get people to do so. You must create a necessity for people to take this communication and expand it to their network. Latham Arneson reveals that one of the worst things you can do is go and ask people outright to tag their friends. Your job as a marketer is to give people a reason to involve others, not just to tell them what to do. Ask yourself why they would want to bring people they know into the conversation.

Posing a question to your audience is always a good strategy. Paramount Pictures will often ask fans to tag friends who remind them of certain characters in a movie trailer they're promoting. It's broad, relatable, and allows the audience to easily involve their friends. Be context specific with your call to actions. Make sure they correlate to the actual content and are interwoven in a creative way.

With scary movies, for example, Arneson's team created a sort of game when they asked fans to tag the friend that would be most terrified of the movie trailer. People like to see their friends get scared—it makes them laugh. Or with romantic movie trailers, asking, "Whom would you most want to experience this story with?" gives people an emotional and sweet reason to bring their lovers into the mix.

Whenever Arneson's team pushed an ad directly asking people to take an action, like to buy tickets, those ads were shared the least. And, not to teach you how to be manipulative or anything, but if you want someone to do something for you, make it seem like you're helping them do what *they* already want to do. Don't ask them outright to do what you want them to do. Let them do things their own way. Don't ask them to share. Make them want to share.

Give It Up Fast

Unlike the dating world, in social media you need to give it up fast. Show your audience the goods! Brownstein explains that his team creates videos that reveal a ton in the beginning. He wants people to lean forward and think, "Oh, what's this goin' to be?" so that they stay interested and want to watch till the end to see how the rest plays out. Letting the viewer in on the gag, for example, helps them feel like they're part of playing the prank.

Julius Dein also explains that he tries to hook his audience within the first three or four seconds of the video, making sure something exciting and interesting happens right away. He suggests keeping the introductions to a minimum and making the video fast paced and engaging. Recently on Facebook, movie studios have also started adopting this approach. They create five-second movie trailers that play before the full movie trailer to more quickly capture their audiences' attention.

Highly Produced Content Is Not Necessarily Shareable

People make the mistake of spending a lot of money on videos with high production value, thinking that because it's well done it will resonate and get shared. Brownstein has observed that some people equate great content with shareable content, but in reality there's not necessarily a correlation. The content needs to go a step further than good or great and connect with the audience emotionally to take the big step to share it.

He illustrates this concept with an example of the award-winning campaign Shareability did for Hyatt. The behind-the-scenes footage for Dua Lipa's "New Rules" music video is the second most successful video on Hyatt's YouTube page and the engagement is through the roof, but when you look at Hyatt's other videos you see that the engagement is really low. The videos are well made and interesting but were not designed to be engaging. They were designed to do a good job of telling a story, but that doesn't inherently make them shareable.

Producer Jon Jashni backs up this idea by explaining that you must think about whom you're creating for from the conception and design stage:

You can't have the creative be the only thing you're focusing on, lest you make something great for you that isn't as appealing to enough people to warrant the cost of creation. But conversely, you can't make something that is noise and fury signifying nothing, where it's all flash and style with no substance—tasty but not nutritious. You've got to serve both masters simultaneously. It has to be something that's appealing.

You need to have the end goal in mind from the beginning. Start by asking yourself what you're trying to achieve so that it's reflected in the way you design the content. If you want your posts to get shared, think about their shareability factor from the start.

Have a Clear Message

Shareable content needs to have a really clear message and narrative. Arneson explains that people must understand what you're giving them or they won't pay attention. He urges content creators to be clear about what they're presenting. He clarifies that you can confuse the viewer in terms of "I don't know what this is, but I'm intrigued" as long as you're intentional. Understand what you're trying to give to the audience so the message resonates. This will make your content more relatable and shareable. Find a way to get the audience to care.

To reflect on what your overall message is, go back to Prince Ea's advice and ask yourself, "If this is the last video I'm ever going to produce, what do I want to say?" That way you can frame the content in a way that's deep and real. As Prince Ea says, "What comes from the heart, reaches the heart."

Quick Tips and Recap

- Shareable content is the number one way to grow quickly and keep fans engaged.

- Serve others. Being service minded will get you further than thinking about yourself. Always try to give to others and think about them first.

- Using a good headline will up your shareability factor because it helps the messaging become clearer and your audience will be more likely to look at the content.

- Connect with your audiences through emotions. Make sure your content makes your audience feel something. Whether it gets them to laugh, cry, or feel in any way, try to reach the audience at the heart level.

- Don't assume that people are watching your videos with sound. It's always good to subtitle your content and ensure that your message is crystal clear.

- Keep video introductions to a minimum. Go straight into something fast paced and exciting. Remember that you only have a second (or three max) to hook someone and grab their interest.

- Play into the unexpected. Have twists, especially at the end of videos.

- Don't force an obvious call to action. Get your audience to share by giving them a reason to involve their friends, not by saying something obvious like "Follow me!" or "Go check this out!" Think of something creative and fun to engage people into performing a specific action.

- Each piece of content should stand on its own. Don't rely on the fact that everyone has seen all your content. Even if they have, you can't expect them to remember what they saw before.

- Don't be afraid to create content or leverage content that's *related* to your subject and not necessarily *about* your subject. Content that shares moments from your brand's lifestyle can be just as powerful. (And when in doubt, sunsets and videos of dolphins surfing work like a charm.)

- Follow your gut and be authentic. Social media is a two-way conversation. When you're genuine and connected to yourself, it's easier for others to connect with you.

CHAPTER 6

STRATEGIC ALLIANCES

C reating strategic partnerships can help you scale very quickly. They're especially helpful if you have less money to spend to grow your platform or want to grow using pure organic strategies. They allow you to go where the audience already exists so you don't have to start from scratch. You just need to figure out what it takes to identify and form the right partnerships that will scale your brand quickly. Generating a big following with the tools I've given you so far can definitely help you stand out and be desirable for potential partners, but there are many other ways. This chapter will help you think outside the box.

Alliances have been the key to success for some of the biggest social media influencers that exist. Julius Dein, magician and social media entrepreneur, attributes his success to partnerships. He started off with a "share-for-share" strategy, where he'd share other people's content on Facebook and they'd share his content in return. He reached out to as many big pages as he could and did favors for them. When he was first starting out, he even paid some to let him feature his posts on their pages. These strategies helped jump-start the growth of his Facebook page, which now has 13.8 million followers, as well as his Instagram, which now has more than 3.2 million followers.

How to Find and Connect with Partners

Understanding your targeting goals helps you choose the right partners. If you know which audience you need to reach, the next step is figuring out the accounts, brands, and people that share the same customers or audience. For example, if you're a women's clothing brand, targeting women between eighteen and thirty-five years old, figure out who else has that audience—find existing influencers and platforms that are targeting that same demographic.

Once you've selected the people you want to create alliances with, you've got to be persistent. Even if you get rejected the first time you reach out, don't give up. Put yourself in the other person's shoes and think about what you would like to receive. Even if someone seems way above your level of influence, you probably still have something useful to offer. *Think about what makes you unique.*

Another important tactic is to focus on forging relationships with superconnectors—people who are attainable and that are connected to a lot of other people. You go to them because they know the people you want to be connected with. Find those in your industry that can connect you to the partners you want to meet. For example, if you want to collaborate with Taylor Swift, you're probably not going to get ahold of her directly. You have to find people who already know her. I wouldn't have worked with Taylor Swift if I hadn't had a preexisting relationship with MTV.

Find your potential collaborator's trusted advisers. MTV's not the only way to get to Taylor Swift. She also has parents, friends, managers, directors, and dancers she's worked with. There are many different ways of getting to people. Reaching out to big stars directly might not resonate. You need a plan.

It's also smart to start by shooting for people closer to your level. If you're opening a boutique clothing store, it's likely that there are influencers in your own town. You don't have to get Kim Kardashian to work with you to have success. There's probably a style icon or fashion blogger in your community that you can partner with. (If you are a local business or brand, I provide additional strategies on how to find and reach out to local influencers in the Instagram chapter.)

Use Whatever You've Got

Sometimes the path to where you want to go isn't direct. There's an actor named Zoë Bell who started out as a stuntwoman. She worked on a ton of Quentin Tarantino's films and was the stuntwoman for Uma Thurman in *Kill Bill*. She was working with Tarantino so often that he ended up casting her in a leading role in his 2007 movie *Death Proof*. Though Bell started in stunt work, she provided something of value, fostered a relationship with one of the top directors in Hollywood, and got into acting in an unexpected way.

David Leitch's story is similar. Originally a stuntman in films such as *V for Vendetta*, *Fight Club*, *300*, and *The Bourne Supremacy*, he fostered relationships and went on to become a second unit director. Eventually, he directed *John Wick*, *Atomic Blonde*, and *Deadpool 2*.

What's the moral of the story here? Sign up for stunt class? No. Ask yourself what you can offer of value to influential people in your industry.

Stand out, get noticed, and be different. And what you can offer doesn't necessarily have to be the exact thing you're trying to do. Something as simple as being a runner or an extra in another influencer's content could lead to future content collaboration. The bottom line is that providing value to influential people in your industry allows you to start an authentic relationship with them. It gets you on their radar, and as the relationship builds, the likelihood that they'll want to help you or leverage your talents increases dramatically.

One or Two Will Do

When Joivan Wade, creator of the Facebook page "The Wall of Comedy!" with 4.2 million followers, started his first web series, he messaged every Facebook connection he had, asking, "Hey, I know you're probably busy, but would you mind checking out my online series?" Some of those people have recently written back, "Oh, Joivan, I see that you've just done your first Hollywood movie. I'm so proud of you, you're doing so well." In the Facebook message chain remains the prior message he sent. Those same people hadn't responded until seven years later to tell him how proud they were. Only about five of the thousands of people he messaged had written back to him right away.

Not everyone has the time or necessity to help or work with you. But you need to keep pushing until you get the results that you want. In other words, don't message five people and get discouraged if none of them respond. Message a hundred more people, and then another hundred people after that until you find people who will advocate for you or the right collaborators to work with. Even if only two or three people want to work with you, it's something. It's quality, not quantity, that helps you grow. Focus on one or two valuable connections or partnerships.

Unique Offerings

Shazam (recently acquired by Apple) is a perfect example of a company that started small with a unique offering, an app that can identify music based on a short sample played using a device's microphone. Chris Barton, Shazam's founder and board director and former head of Android business development for Google, has always focused on partnership business development to accelerate growth. Barton explains that in the beginning Shazam struggled for six years before it had any success. It was a small start-up that built its platform before smartphones even had apps on them. Then, finally, Shazam entered into a partnership with AT&T to distribute a music recognition application that generated significant revenues for Shazam in those nascent start-up days. Even though its scale paled in comparison, Shazam's technology was valuable to AT&T, offering the ability to differentiate its phones from other phone company providers. And the money that Shazam got from this partnership helped the start-up further develop its technology.

The AT&T deal was not Shazam branded, meaning Shazam didn't get its brand's name attached to the technology on the AT&T platform. So Barton and his team still wanted to find an opportunity to grow brand awareness and expand the company. When the iPhone came out in 2007, the App Store didn't yet exist. Barton's team thought, "Wouldn't it be great if we could get Shazam on the iPhone?" In 2008 Apple started to put together the App Store for launch. They reached out to a handful of companies and Shazam was among them. This "luck," said Barton, was due to the fact that their product had a unique offering.

That's when Shazam's scaling to massive audiences began. Back then there were only one or two million iPhones—not the crazy numbers you see today—but for Shazam it was game changing. People were downloading their apps, and as the number of iPhone sales increased, so did Shazam downloads.

Barton says that what really led to Shazam becoming a massive success was the combination of the accessibility through the iPhone app platform, coupled with a simple but great user experience. It was almost magical for people to discover that they could push a button and immediately find out the names of songs. It delighted users so much that they would end up showing the app to their friends, which drove massive word-of-mouth growth. So if you have a unique offering and can find the right partners, you can position yourself for massive growth.

YouTube is another company that grew because of its offering and a strategic alliance. It was built and acquired in twenty-two months for $1.6 billion because it strategically leveraged the Myspace platform to direct traffic to its own platform. YouTube created a snippet of code (now referred to as an embed code) so people could embed videos into their Myspace profiles. This was novel at the time; it acted as Myspace's first video player. When users saw that their friends were embedding videos on their Myspace profiles, they often wanted to follow suit. YouTube grew because it was seen on Myspace profiles, and users were sharing the word about the company without even realizing it.

YouTube also made some intelligent moves like having its logo on the player and designing it so that when users clicked on the video it took them to the YouTube website. It's important to note that this is a different kind of strategic "alliance" because Myspace actually didn't even know this was occurring at first. By the time YouTube gained critical mass and Myspace tried to stop it, it was too late. Myspace responded to YouTube's tremendous growth, when it finally noticed it, by deactivating YouTube's embed code, which caused Myspace users to revolt, forcing Myspace to reactivate it. Then Myspace tried to acquire YouTube but lost out to Google. So sometimes you can maximize the value of traffic sources from social and digital platforms without having to create "formal" partnerships. In this case, for example, YouTube leveraged the fact that Myspace already allowed embed codes on users' profiles to build their audiences. Instagram also scaled quickly by encouraging people to share their beautiful pictures on their Facebook profiles, which drew more users to the Instagram platform. Though Facebook was aware of it, the two platforms didn't have any kind of formal partnership until Facebook acquired Instagram in 2012.

Zenga took a similar approach by leveraging Facebook's platform when it started in 2001. At the time, Facebook allowed game users to send friends invites like "This person wants to invite you to play . . ." Facebook eventually changed the way you could send invites, but by that time Zenga had already leveraged this tool to grow into a billion-dollar company.

Barton also pointed out that Dropbox, where he served as head of mobile business development, is another example of a company whose growth is attributed to partnerships. Dropbox tried every imaginable tactic to drive growth. Eventually what worked best for them was getting users to invite their friends by gifting free storage. Essentially, Dropbox structured a partnership with their users.

Strategic alliances work. They're what got me Taylor Swift and Rihanna as clients. I partnered with MTV on a platform I'd built and then MTV introduced me to Taylor Swift and other big celebrities. As long as you capitalize on your unique offerings, you'll be amazed by the access you can have to the right people who will help you grow.

Gifting

Gifting is another strategy many brands use to build partnerships (especially out here in Hollywood). Brands pay to get into gifting suites, which allow them to get their product in the hands of celebrities. You have to give your product to the celebrities for free, but you can get pictures of them using or holding it, which exposes your product to a larger audience and gives the product more credibility in the eyes of fans.

Writing Featured Articles

You don't have to be an app inventor or techie or even be selling products to make strategic partnerships work for you. You just need to figure out who needs your skills.

Perhaps you're a fashion blogger or a fashion designer. In this case, you could do a featured article for another, slightly bigger (or huge) fashion blog. Just make sure you find someone with an audience that matches your target. You can offer to write a free article every week for a month as long as your target uses your name and links back to your website. This will expose your brand, platform, or products to other people.

Identify and Provide Value to People with Traffic

When I worked for film production and finance company Lakeshore Entertainment, I wanted to form partnerships with movie bloggers. At the time, most film bloggers weren't taken seriously, except for Harry Knowles, who founded and ran Ain't It Cool News. He was the only person that people in the movie industry wanted to work with, but they still didn't really treat him with respect. They just expected him to put their content on his blog.

To change this dynamic and create better alliances with movie bloggers, our team started hosting private parties where movie talent, like actors and directors, would come and hang out with bloggers. We treated the bloggers like rock stars and friends. We made them feel included in the process. Additionally, we gave them exclusive content. For example, when working with actor Jason Statham on the 2006 movie *Crank*, we recorded custom video introductions for the top movie bloggers for the release of the movie.

We used these tactics because we knew that the movie bloggers had big audiences and the studio I was working for was dealing with smaller marketing budgets, of around $15 to $30 million per movie. It may sound like a lot, but it's nothing compared to the $50 to $100 million marketing budgets of big studio releases. Our team had to find intelligent ways to stand out and market our films. By creating partnerships with the movie bloggers, we established relationships that got more people to pay attention to our content.

Now I am not saying you have to go out and throw big crazy parties. You just need to identify who is influential and who has a large audience in your industry and then show them as much genuine attention as possible.

Collaborating

Collaborating with the right people helps build and foster your audience. If you're a musician, you can offer influencers free use of your music for their videos. If you're a model, you can contact every big Instagram photographer in your niche and tell them that you'll work on their next brand campaign for free. If you're an athlete, you can collaborate with other athletes. For example, pro surfer Coco Ho and her boyfriend, professional snowboarder Mark McMorris, often posted about each other on Instagram and Facebook, which built and drove each of their respective audiences to each other's social channels. You-Tube success is always greatly enhanced by collaboration and pushing fans toward each other (we will dive deeper into this in chapter nine).

To make these relationships thrive, it's all about social dynamics. Create partnerships that are mutually beneficial on both sides. Use strategic collaborations and partnerships to fuel and grow your brand.

Dua Lipa / Hyatt Collaboration

Erick Brownstein, president and chief strategy officer at Shareability, worked on an award-winning collaboration between singer-songwriter Dua Lipa and Hyatt Hotels Corporation.[1] Hyatt came to Shareability explaining that they had wanted to do something related to music for a long time but hadn't found the right act. Shareability suggested underwriting the music video

[1] "Dua Lipa's New Rules Music Video, The Confidante Miami Beach Part of the Unbound Collection by Hyatt, Winner in YouTube Partnership," 10th Annual Shorty Awards, http://shortyawards.com/10th/dua-lipa-new-rules.

of a cool, up-and-coming artist. In exchange, they'd shoot the music video at one of the Hyatt locations that they wanted to promote. The hotel would be the backdrop and the context for the video. And they'd shoot a bunch of behind-the-scenes content in the hotel that could be launched on Hyatt's YouTube channel.

Hyatt went forward with the idea and chose the Confidante Hotel in Miami Beach. As part of the Unbound Collection by Hyatt, where trendsetting boutique and independent hotels team up with Hyatt management, the Confidante isn't actually a Hyatt-branded hotel, but corporate wanted to appeal to a younger demographic, so it was a good choice. Shareability chose to work with Dua Lipa, who was just starting to take off. She had international appeal and was attractive to a young audience. They approached her, told her the plan, and she agreed.

The first three seconds of the "New Rules" music video is the only part that shows the whole hotel and its name. And then each scene of the music video takes place in the hotel—the bedrooms, the hallways, the pool, the restaurant, and the cabana. Shareability made sure to give the viewer the whole hotel experience.

"New Rules" currently has nearly 1.2 billion views. Lipa's popularity went soaring from thirteen million streams a month to four million a day. The video completely exploded her career. And the behind-the-scenes footage currently has more than twenty million views on Hyatt's channels.

This collaboration was highly beneficial for both parties. Hyatt is recognized now by the labels in the recording industry as the perfect partner to work with for new artists. Hyatt and the Confidante have also since been featured in articles in music magazines as big as *Rolling Stone* and *Billboard*. And every article about the successful music video mentions "Dua Lipa at the Confidante Hotel in Miami Beach." The hotel has received incredible exposure as the costar of the video.

Think About the Headline Your Partnership Creates

Latham Arneson, former VP of digital marketing for Paramount Pictures, explains that movie studios regularly use strategic partnerships to help get messages and brand awareness out in larger ways.

Sometimes his team thinks about the kind of headline that a strategic partnership can create—one that people will pay attention to and that fits within the narrative of the film. Studio executives always want to create something that helps people engage deeper with their brand and that actually gets them to go see the movie or engage with the content.

One time, Arneson worked on a partnership between Uber and the 2014 movie *Transformers: Age of Extinction*. People could order a ride in Optimus Prime, a fictional Autobot character from the *Transformers* series, through Uber in three or four major cities in the United States. It played into the movie's themes because of the relationships between humans and the alien robots that can disguise themselves as cars. It was a unique and creative partnership that received a lot of interest and benefited both companies.

Before creating a partnership, Arneson suggests asking yourself two questions: (1) Is anyone going to pay attention to the activity or partnership? and (2) Does the partnership *elevate your brand*—does it get people to engage or take action in any way? Those are the critical components. You can think of kitschy ideas, but if they don't actually help your brand, they're not useful. Viral activity for the sake of virality doesn't mean anything. It has to *enhance* whatever message or purpose you're trying to achieve.

Influencer Platforms

One way to find relevant influencers for your brand is by using an influencer platform like CreatorIQ, Speakr, or Traackr. Influencer platforms allow you to run searches with various variables. They can help you build engagement groups or you can pay top influencers to like and comment on your photos to help them go viral. You can also use these platforms if you want to promote yourself as an influencer and find potential brands with which to collaborate.

To choose the right influencers, you need to think about your company's goals and who your customers are. Then you can make a list of the people who will best help you reach that audience. On the influencer platforms, you can search by influencer categories such as business, finance, travel, skincare, food and drinks, and the like. There are categories related to all fields. You can also break them down by location, platform, brand, celebrity, post frequency, profile type, recent posts, how many followers they have, and so on.

Keep in mind that you need to continuously test and try different influencers. David Oh explains that over the years his team has tested more than five thousand different influencers to find the ones that yield the highest returns. Not every influencer is going to deliver and perform for your brand. Just because they have an audience of millions doesn't mean you will automatically make millions from that collaboration. It's all about testing and finding the right fit.

Share and Engagement Groups

Share and engagement groups are a great form of partnering for growing fast organically. Joivan Wade, founder of the Facebook page "The Wall of Comedy!" leveraged the engagement group strategy as an important part of his page's growth and his content's virality. His company has created a share network with different pages and platforms. When a member of the network creates a piece of content, they send it out to all the people in the network who can then share the content on their pages, like and comment on the content on the original creator's page, or both. On Instagram, for example, someone can upload a video or picture and then five people who have large followings from the share network like or comment on it. This gives the content a much higher chance of hitting Instagram's Explore page, which helps boost its visibility and gives the original poster the opportunity to generate a significant amount of impressions, which subsequently leads to more followers.

Content is exposed to a larger audience by developing a community with people who interchange sharing each other's posts. Wade cites the example of the virality of Michael Dapaah's character Big Shaq. He says that it became a viral sensation mainly owing to a mass amount of big social accounts sharing it at the same time—the velocity of these shares made it go viral.

You can't assume that sharing content with your own audience is enough. Be strategic and find partners. That way you can collectively come together in a supportive group and push each other's content. Find accounts, pages, and people that are in a similar space as you. If you're a comedian, find other comedians. If you're an artist, find other artists. If you're a photographer, find other photographers. Reach out to your peers and ask if they would like to partner and be in an engagement group with you. Or perhaps they're already part of an engagement group that you can join. By working together you'll have more success.

Leveraging Other People's Content to Grow Fast

Wade grew his Facebook page "The Wall of Comedy!" to 4.2 million followers in under two years, and currently it generates over 350 million views per month. All this growth has been organic; his team has never spent a penny on advertising. From Wade's perspective, advertising dollars aren't necessary if you have creative zest and the right ideas.

One of the brilliant facts about his Facebook page is that 70 percent of the content is licensed and only 30 percent is original. He's leveraged other people's content to help build an audience so that later his team could go back and push their own original content to that same audience. It's also important to note that Wade's not paying for the licensed content—he's simply offering video creators the ability to reach the huge audience he has built, which generates exposure for them as creators. This is a smart way to marry my system with an organic strategy. Build a massive following and then approach content partners to license their content for free in exchange for exposing their brand to your newly built audience.

Netflix is a perfect example of a company that employed a similar strategy. It originally started with a group of popular licensed content that people already loved, with TV series like *The Fresh Prince of Bel-Air* and Disney movies. Netflix brought viewers to a hub where they could watch all their favorite shows and flicks, which made it easy to build an audience. And once that audience was large enough, Netflix created and released original content.

When that original content came out . . . *bam!* There was a ready-made audience for it, which gave them leverage to release shows of the magnitude of *House of Cards* and *Orange Is the New Black*. Would they have been as successful without Netflix's built-in audience? It's hard to say for certain, but we do know that Netflix had been building their customer base through licensed content for more than fifteen years before they released those original programs.

Jukin Media, known as the Getty Images for viral videos, has created a very lucrative business because of content leveraging.

Jukin licenses viral user-generated videos from all over the world. It supplies content from its channels and massive library to other people so they can leverage it to build their brands. Jukin's library of content includes hilarious fail clips (e.g., people falling off things, playing pranks), pet videos, and videos of people doing amazing things (e.g., backflips, remarkable stunts). It works with some of the biggest TV shows and media companies in the world and some of the biggest digital publishers and websites, including AOL, the *Huffington Post*, and Yahoo! The idea behind the company is that you can rewatch the same video many times; content can be repackaged and repurposed. Jukin has figured out a way to extend the lifetime value of content, which helps brands as it's really hard to create content from scratch because of the high costs associated with filmmaking. Between YouTube and Facebook, it currently has about eighty million followers, which has all been built by leveraging the power of found footage and authentic content created by other creators. Jukin's team members have become experts and have collected data about which types of content go viral organically.

Whether you're running a company that's struggling to generate significant engagement on social platforms or someone who's building a personal brand from scratch, you can partner with other people or brands, license and leverage others' content, or join share and engagement groups to get a more well-rounded content-strategy approach. You can still prioritize and push your original content but also leverage the power of strategic alliances to significantly grow your audience and engagement.

Quick Tips and Recap

- Strategic alliances can take you to where an audience already exists so you don't have to start from scratch.

- Partnerships help get messages and brand awareness out there in larger ways.

- Find strategic partnerships that drive growth. You want quality, not quantity.

- Find the superconnectors you can reach that will connect you to other people.

- Put yourself in your partners' shoes to think about what could be valuable to them.

- Be creative when approaching partners. Think about your unique offering and how it matches with the needs of the person you're approaching.

- Work on a share-for-share basis.

- At first, look for partners who are attainable—they don't have to have a much larger following than you to help you.

- Create or join engagement groups where you share and create content with others. Content goes viral because a huge number of people share something at the same time.

- Look for headline-grabbing partnerships.

- Licensing other people's content is a good, cost-effective strategy to help you grow.

- Build a massive following and then approach content partners to license their content for free in exchange for exposing their brands to your newly built audience.

CHAPTER 7

GO GLOBAL (AN OPPORTUNITY)

G oing global can be extremely valuable. Today there are 323 million people in the United States, yet there are 7.6 billion people in the world. The biggest celebrities and influencers always have a global plan for building an audience in other countries—it's a great way to scale into a true megastar.

Emmy Award–winning producer Mike Jurkovac agrees. He says that the Black Eyed Peas became one of the biggest bands in the world because they knew how to connect with an international audience. When they went to Brazil, will.i.am would wear the national team's soccer jersey. When they were in Mexico, Taboo would have a Mexican flag. They are the only group in the world that has sold out the Stade de France, all eighty thousand seats, three times. Even Jay-Z envied their success, saying, "If I was as big as you guys are outside of the United States, I'd be really happy." If you understand how to leverage a worldwide audience, it can significantly broaden your opportunities both across the globe and on your home turf.

I'd like to point out, however, that although going global provides an amazing opportunity, it's not necessarily right for everyone. Through the extensive testing I have conducted in research for this book, I find that emerging markets are the next big thing in social and digital in terms of scale. But if you're an e-commerce company that only sells to the US market, then going global is not a top priority and you're not going to need to acquire an audience and followers in emerging markets.

However, even if you don't sell products abroad, having a worldwide audience can still help build up your validation and credibility metrics. Having a large following, regardless of where the followers come from, gets people to take you more seriously. Going global is often a great opportunity to scale very quickly in a short period that also allows you to be unique and stand out.

Country borders especially don't matter as much if you're an actor, director, musician, or artist. A musician can sell music anywhere. *American Idol* finalist Jasmine Trias only sold fourteen thousand copies of her album in the United States but went platinum in the Philippines. If she hadn't thought globally, she would have missed a huge opportunity to continue her dream of being a professional singer. And if you're an actor, keep in mind that 60 to 70 percent of box office revenue is generated overseas, meaning international sales are actually more significant than domestic ones. If you can walk into a studio or casting director's office and say, "You know, India is the third largest box office market in the world with $1.9 billion in sales a year.[1] And I have X number of followers there," that

---

[1] "Theatrical Market Statistics 2016," Motion Picture Association of America, https://www.mpaa.org/wp-content/uploads/2017/03/MPAA-Theatrical-Market -Statistics-2016_Final.pdf.

should make you stand out and give you some clout. If you have an audience in valuable international markets such as Mexico, Brazil, India, Indonesia, Poland, or Turkey it can absolutely help separate you from the crowd and at the very least make you look smart and driven. The film industry is making a lot of money off those territories, and some films only survive because of their international box office numbers.

Seeing the Opportunities in Other Parts of the World

As I mentioned earlier, there are 7.6 billion people in the world. Too many businesses focus too narrowly and end up ignoring people from other countries. I always advocate standing out and being different from everyone else, which is harder to do in the United States or the United Kingdom because so many people are fighting over an audience in these markets. Even if you're a creative genius and have something truly remarkable to offer, it's hard to get attention without widening your scope.

People think that having the market share in the United States, United Kingdom, and Canada is more valuable than having it in other parts of the world. It's true that your valuation skyrockets dramatically when you have an audience in these regions, but you shouldn't discount opportunities in other locations. I recommend testing your content or brand in different markets that are not oversaturated and that have less competition.

WhatsApp is a perfect example of a successful company that did just that. They had tremendous success capturing large shares of Malaysia, Turkey, Saudi Arabia, India, and Brazil. Most people would automatically discredit those countries or deem them irrelevant. WhatsApp, on the other hand, grew and scaled those audiences. The team behind WhatsApp built the company up until it was eventually acquired for $17 billion, which is one of the largest tech acquisitions of our time.

One of the main reasons Facebook bought WhatsApp was its international audience. Facebook already had enough customers in the "higher-value" markets of the United States, United Kingdom, and Canada. It needed an opportunity to extend its reach and scale to other parts of the world.

Cost Efficiency

On the Facebook advertising platform, it's currently much more cost efficient to reach people in emerging markets. Acquiring a follower or a like in India, Indonesia, Brazil, or Mexico is far cheaper than targeting people in the United States. This is because there are not a lot of people fighting over those countries, which creates an excess of inventory in the auction. Fewer people bid on those areas, and thus the cost to acquire or engage users is very low. This presents a huge opportunity to scale a massive global audience.

Acquiring a follower in India, or some of the other emerging markets, can cost less than a penny, whereas if you're trying to get a follower in the States, it can cost around seven to ten cents. Again, that fluctuates based on the quality of your content, but it presents a big opportunity.

Emerging Markets First

A highly effective strategy to build up your following or engagement on a post is to focus on sending it out to emerging markets first. Emerging markets are cheaper and have a propensity to like and share at a higher velocity. Then, once the post has picked up traction in these regions, you reroute the post to your target audience in domestic markets.

This works because of perceived value and credibility. Imagine you have two pieces of content that come into your feed. One has ten thousand likes and the other has five likes. Which one are you going to take more seriously? You'll probably be more attracted to the one with higher engagement, even if it was the exact same post. Generally, it's easier to get people to engage with a piece of content that ten thousand people have liked because the content looks more valuable to the viewer.

I tend to build engagement in less expensive markets first. I've been able to get a hundred thousand people to like a photo in the emerging markets because of low costs and high engagement. Afterward, I go back and retarget people in the higher-cost countries. This also allows me to get more engagement at a much lower cost in the competitive markets because I have found that this helps reduce the cost in the auction. If a piece of content generates a significant amount of engagement, the Facebook algorithm sees that the content is good and allows one to bid cheaper in the United States, United Kingdom, and Canada, regardless of where the original engagement comes from. (This may change in the future if people working at Facebook read this book, so get on it while you still can.)

Inexpensive Yet Valuable Countries

On the Facebook advertising platform, India and Indonesia are the cheapest countries to target that drive significant engagement. Many countries in Africa are also very inexpensive; however, I don't put a lot of focus there because it usually hasn't been as valuable for returns for my clients. With that said, there are large brands that are investing heavily in Africa because of the tremendous scale. Brazil and Mexico are also cost effective with high engagement.

I find that India is a country that presents tremendous opportunity. Even though it has a low GDP, the population is very large with more than 1.3 billion people. It's the country with the second-largest population in the world. Seeing the same opportunity for growth there, IKEA is investing $2 billion over the next fifteen to twenty years to open twenty-five new stores throughout India. And Rupert Murdoch's company just paid $2.6 billion to win against Facebook's bid of $600 million for exclusive rights to broadcast India's cricket games. Facebook also announced in 2017 that India has become their number one country audience in the world with 251 million users.[2] If Facebook can acquire the other billion people in the country over the next five to ten years, that would represent 50 percent of their total user base today. As you can see, some very smart people have their focus on India since it presents large growth opportunities at a cost-efficient rate.

---

[2] Simon Kemp, "India Overtakes the USA to Become Facebook's #1 Country," The Next Web, July 13, 2017, https://thenextweb.com/contributors/2017/07/13/india-overtakes-usa-become-facebooks-top-country.

If you want people to really share your content, however, I recommend testing in Brazil. While working with professional surfers, I learned that Brazil has a very big sharing culture. Brazilians online seem to share content like no other community. Tim Greenberg, chief community officer at the World Surf League, agrees. When Brazilian professional surfer Gabriel Medina won the world title, the World Surf League generated a lot of followers and growth because of Medina's home fans.

Importance of Global for Shazam

Chris Barton, founder and board director of Shazam, explains that when they initially launched, the United States was not ready for a "Shazam-like experience." Europe happened to be more advanced in mobile technology at the time and the company continues to be significantly more popular in Europe on a per capita basis than it is in the States. Today, Shazam's users come from all over the world. The company is popular in Latin America, Canada, Australia, Brazil, Mexico, India, Russia, and some parts of Asia. Barton feels that if you want to achieve a maximum scale of users, then you absolutely need to factor in emerging markets.

He warns, however, that emerging markets aren't always easy to break in to. He has seen that local competitors will often outdo foreigners in those markets because they do a better job of localizing the business. So if you want to include emerging markets in your business, do your research and be smart about it.

The Power of International Markets for Growth

If you have a product that can extend to other markets, look at global growth opportunities—pay attention to them, consider them, and put them on your road map. Eamonn Carey, an early-stage angel investor, has invested in more than thirty-one companies around the world. He's worked with organizations as large as AB InBev and Nike; scaled businesses in the United Kingdom, the Middle East, and Asia; cofounded and sold a parody version of *FarmVille* called *Farm-Villain* in Europe and the Middle East; and is currently the managing director of the London branch of Techstars, a worldwide network that helps entrepreneurs succeed. He loves working with early-stage companies that have big plans and ambitions, hoping to help them get somewhere interesting. With all his experience he's a huge advocate of investing in and bringing companies to emerging markets.

He explains that as an investor it's frequently an awful lot easier, and always an awful lot cheaper, to invest in companies in emerging markets. The companies that he's invested in out of New York, for example, need a minimum of $1 million, usually closer to $3 million, to keep themselves going for around eighteen months. Recently, however, he was in Bangalore, India, meeting with a very smart six-person team working in artificial intelligence who needed only $150,000 dollars to keep themselves going for the same amount of time. From an investment value point of view, you can often do deals a lot more cheaply in these markets.

He also pointed out that times have changed. Ten years ago it wasn't the case, but today the companies he invests in, whether located in the United States or India, have a similar quality level. He attributes this to better access to education. Almost everyone in the world can use Harvard CS 101, look on iTunes University, Corsair, or U-2-Me. Broader access to education has raised business quality across the world.

The second big thing Carey notes is the scale of emerging markets. A media company he developed created Arabic travel guides for cities in the Middle East. Arabic is the fifth-most spoken language in the world.[3] However, less than 0.5 percent of internet content is in Arabic. This discrepancy points out a huge opportunity. Hundreds of millions of Arabic speakers across the Middle East and North Africa aren't seeing enough content in their own language.

And this scale of opportunity is not unique to those regions. Indonesia has 250 million people, India 1.3 billion, and Japan has 127 million. Thailand and Malaysia each have tens of millions. Vietnam has nearly a hundred million. A lot of emerging markets are huge. If a company can take the best business practices from the United States and Europe and combine them with local knowledge, there's a major opening for success.

As mentioned before, the cost per acquisition can be very expensive in the States and the United Kingdom, while in Saudi Arabia, India, Ukraine, Russia, or Latin America the cost per acquisition of a follower is frequently less than a cent. The same applies for the cost of other key performance indicators (i.e., cost per lead, cost per share, cost per link click, and cost per conversion). A lot of people will point out that you won't make as much revenue from users in other parts of the world as you will from users in wealthier countries. Carey agrees that although this may be true, you must consider your ROI. If you're acquiring users at a fraction of the cost, it may not be significant that you're generating a smaller amount of revenue—just be sure that the proportions are working in your favor.

Carey gives the example of a company he worked with named Wala. It was a new bank that wanted to open in Ghana. The com-

---

[3] Vivek Kumar Singh, "Most Spoken Languages in the World," ListsWorld, November 10, 2012, http://www.listsworld.com/top-10-languages-most-spoken -worldwide.

pany effectively built a massive Facebook community for hardly any money at all. It only spent a couple of thousand dollars on ads, and because the cost per acquisition was so low it reached half a million people very quickly. When members of Wala's team went and talked to investors and partners, they were able to show them their large Facebook community. They had been posting relevant content about finance and financial inclusion, which were areas of interest to this community. All Wala needed to do was convert a very small percentage of its following to actual bank accounts, and they'd be one of the top ten banks in the country overnight.

Stories like that make you realize that you can do things in emerging markets that would cost you millions of dollars in the United States to achieve. When you look at it this way, emerging markets suddenly start to become a lot more viable.

Investing Abroad Makes You Stand Out

Carey shares that if you're pitching a US, UK, Canadian, or German company in Indonesia, Thailand, or Vietnam, you're so unusual that you'll get better quality meetings with more senior people and have a better opportunity to close deals. One time, Carey invested in a company called Paranoid Fan, a sports and entertainment mapping company that shows you where the shortest queue for the restroom is, where tailgate parties are happening, and other interesting things related to sports and entertainment events. The company works with NFL, NBA, and major league soccer teams in the States. Then they got some interest from Mexico and Brazil, so the company went down and did a little miniature road show around Mexico, Brazil, Uruguay, Argentina, and Chile, pitching their B2B and mapping solutions to an array of different clubs. They walked away from that trip with deals with all the major Mexican, Brazilian, Uruguayan, Argentinian, and Chilean football teams, and with a bunch of partnerships with the governing bodies as well. They captured about thirty million users, without ever having to spend a dime on marketing. When Paranoid Fan met with executives on those trips it was praised for being there in person. People in other countries explained that US companies had pitched to them before but only by sending emails asking for conversations by Skype. Going down there and physically meeting people gave Paranoid Fan the opportunity to sign deals quickly.

Later, Paranoid Fan also went to the World Football Summit in Madrid, Spain, and did deals with most of the major European soccer clubs. If it had gone with only two million users, it wouldn't have been as desirable. But the fact that it had thirty million users gave it credibility, and it didn't matter where those users were located.

Retention and Attention

If you target people in Indonesia, India, or Brazil, the engagement is often ten times what you'll see in the United States or the United Kingdom. You're going against fewer competitive sources of content and fewer advertisers from domestic companies. Carey adds that in Brazil, Saudi Arabia, and Middle Eastern markets, people typically spend four times the number of hours per day on their phone than people in Western markets. People in the United States or the United Kingdom may spend forty minutes a day on Facebook, while the average person in Brazil or Saudi Arabia may spend multiple hours. The appetite for fresh and interesting new content, and the propensity to like and share is far greater than in Western markets. This lower barrier of entry makes it easier to catalyze a piece of content to go viral in emerging markets.

Popularity Helps Reach Bigger Markets

When speaking to the founders of Skype, Carey discovered that one of the first international markets they launched in was Taiwan. Although Taiwan is a small island, it has a market of twenty million people with strong links to the billion-people market in China. People there started hearing from their families for free with this new form of voice and video calls. This made Skype go viral immediately.

If you can build an audience in an emerging market, you can very easily start to build an audience in other markets. It's similar to the WhatsApp example in acquiring users in cheaper markets, building up an incredible reputation with them, and then using that popularity to reach bigger markets.

For example, imagine you want to get Coca-Cola as a sponsor or a client in the United States or the United Kingdom. Going directly is often impossible. But if you build up a huge audience in Indonesia, India, or Brazil, it's far easier to strike deals with the head of Coke in those countries, which can then lead to introductions to the executives in the United States or United Kingdom. And if you're doing well in a foreign market, you have proof that your brand or company can drive success. If you're strategic and recognize how to maximize and leverage the potential of building an audience in a specific part of the world, it can help your business immensely.

Many start-ups believe that success equals raising $50 million from a VC fund in Silicon Valley, having a bunch of engineers in an office in San Francisco, and conquering the US market bit by bit. In reality, you can do equally as well in emerging markets for far less money, and the outcomes over time will start to equalize.

Carey says that if you want to solve a problem, think of the best possible outcome and then work backward from there. Ask yourself what steps you need to take to get where you want to go. What are all the potential actions that lead to the point you want to reach? Start mapping out how you get to each one of those. Eventually, a very simple and straightforward path will form. And using the approach of acquiring users, clients, and customers in emerging markets can be an unbelievably powerful tool to get you where you want to go.

Personal Brands

Carey thinks that the opportunities are even larger for personal brands. For example, there are so few live music events and so few artists that go to emerging markets to perform. If you're a musician, the opportunity to get in front of a crowd of five hundred or a thousand people just by being willing to show up is significant. Again, the propensity of foreign markets to share and comment will be of great benefit. Also, if people listen to your music on Spotify in Thailand, Vietnam, Malaysia, or Singapore, the chances of getting featured on Discover Weekly around the world are probably going to start increasing. You'll build up your reputation and internal metrics on these channels. (This can be applied to many other fields as well. Use your brain and make it happen.)

Carey shares that one time he posted a selfie with an Iranian company at a conference in Istanbul. Within twenty-four hours it had been retweeted hundreds of times and liked thousands of times. He had a bunch of Facebook friend requests, LinkedIn messages, and invitations to go and speak at conferences in Iran. The triumvirate of more time, more attention, and more sharing means you can break out more easily. It's a virgin territory where you can get feedback and build a community, and then return home with a hugely engaged fan base. This will make it much easier for you to get a book deal, a record deal, or a movie role. And you'll feel like a rock star no matter what you do.

Today, so many actors are getting knocked back for roles because they don't have enough social media followers. Carey recommends going to Indonesia or another emerging market, making two or three films, and being the most active person on social media by engaging with fans in that territory. Build an audience abroad and then go back and talk to the casting agents in Hollywood or London, showing that you have a million followers. In most cases, people don't really know or ask where your followers come from, just the fact that you have fans automatically makes you stand out from the rest of the crowd. And your value also goes up when you have access to an audience that very few other people have.

Hollywood movie producer, media executive, and investor Jon Jashni adds that when producers are investing at scale they factor in worldwide appeal; the narrower the target, the smaller the returns.

A lot of filmmakers are afraid that speaking one common language will dilute other languages. Or they fear that making something for the masses will take away their cultural identity, but this isn't really the case. "The goal is to highlight the facets of the jewel in such way that the market or territory understands that that story is for them," Jashni says. If you've done your job as a creator, the universality of theme, character, relatability, and emotion will transcend borders.

Good Content Travels Well

Phil Ranta, former COO of Studio71, one of the largest influencer-driven digital entertainment companies, discloses that YouTube is being unlocked in territories where it wasn't previously popular. Digital platforms are truly global; people are starting to discover more content from various cultures. The fact that content is accessible anywhere in the world means that creating with a global audience in mind leads to success.

He suggests trying to create content that's not language-specific. Try to make the joke or the premise understandable without necessarily knowing the language. Another option is to include translations. YouTube has built-in tools that help create closed captions, and if you create them in English YouTube does a good job of translating them to other languages.

Ranta feels that people who aren't thinking globally now are going to struggle in five or ten years. There are many places where internet infrastructure is just starting to pick up; in those locations, people are just now getting mobile phones that can stream content they couldn't access before. All those markets will start growing and developing new fandom.

Jonathan Skogmo, CEO of Jukin Media, agrees. His company has a huge universal and global audience with 75 percent of its three billion monthly views coming from outside the United States. He says, "Good content travels really well. An ouch is an ouch in any language." Jukin Media licenses and distributes a lot of viral comedic fail videos, since a guy falling over is a guy falling over anywhere. His team looks at the global picture of content because they see real scale and value by focusing on different parts of the world where others are simply not paying attention.

Quick Tips and Recap

- Acquiring a follower or a like in India, Indonesia, Brazil, or Mexico is far cheaper than in the States because there aren't a lot of people fighting over those countries, which creates an excess of inventory in the auction.
- Followers in emerging markets can cost less than a penny, versus eight or nine cents in the States.
- In emerging markets, there's often less competition and users spend more time on mobile devices.
- India is an important country; it's where some of the smartest people on the planet are investing, so keep it on your radar.
- Brazil loves to share more than most countries. Test your content against this audience to make content go viral.
- A smart strategy is to build engagement on a piece of content in emerging markets first because of the lower cost

efficiency. Then, once you have significant engagement, share that post with your core target demos in domestic markets. You'll get more engagement at a lower cost.

- If you're a start-up, build a massive audience in emerging markets and then become an attractive acquisition target for a company from the United States or the United Kingdom that's looking to extend its audience. The same applies if you are an individual or a start-up trying to partner with global brands.
- People in other markets appreciate if you go and visit them. It can help you grow.
- Good content travels well. Create content that's not language-specific. Create with global in mind.

CHAPTER 8

GAINING INFLUENCE ON INSTAGRAM

With more than seven hundred million monthly active users, Instagram is a platform that can't be ignored.[1] It's an essential marketing and storytelling tool that gives users a quick, accessible, emotional, and highly visual experience of your brand and messages. It's one reason Instagram has the highest average brand engagement rate of all the main social media channels.[2]

Nevertheless, it isn't the easiest platform on which to achieve rapid growth. One of the biggest differences between Instagram and Facebook is that it's not inherently built as a sharing platform, leaving you with the need to find other ways to make content go viral.

---

[1] "Number of Daily Active Instagram Users from October 2016 to September 2017 (in Millions)," Statista, https://www.statista.com/statistics/657823/number-of-daily-active-instagram-users.

[2] Khalid Saleh, "Social Media Engagement—Statistics and Trends," *Invesp* (blog), https://www.invespcro.com/blog/social-media-engagement.

While Facebook is designed to get you to share, Instagram is primarily designed for you to like, comment, and tag. Success on the platform relies heavily on your ability to leverage strategic partnerships for growth. A lot of the information you've gathered from chapter six, "Strategic Alliances," will be of great use to you to achieve success on this platform.

For real growth, virality, and success on Instagram, your goal is to get people with status to like and comment on your content. On Instagram, status is defined by two metrics: (1) number of followers, and (2) lifetime of an account. Those who've been on the platform longer have more clout. The algorithm is created this way to prevent people from cheating the system. There was a time when some users were rapidly building new sister accounts to lift the weight of their other Instagram accounts (this doesn't work anymore, so don't get any ideas).

Rapid Growth on IG

Getting featured on the Explore page, which is Instagram's general search page, is the best way for content to go viral and for you to be discovered. Getting featured on this page in a large number of people's accounts requires a lot of "power likes"—likes and comments from high-profile accounts with hundreds of thousands or even millions of followers. Each Explore page is tailored to the particular user's interests, but if a super influencer likes your content, it will be more visible to a good number of people.

Adley Stump, a digital marketing strategist, explains that this is because likes grow exponentially. If a verified account with a hundred thousand followers in your niche "likes" your content, Instagram's algorithms will push your post to the majority of those hundred thousand followers' Explore feeds. And that's just one power like—imagine getting a hundred or a thousand power likes. Also, although it's not necessary for the power likes to be niche-specific, it does increase the conversion rate for growth because you'll show up in feeds of people who already show interest in that type of content. It's less valuable to get power likes from someone in the car niche when you're in the pet niche.

One way to get power likes and to reach a lot of Explore pages is by using engagement groups (see chapter six). Using them as a part of your Instagram strategy really helps your content go viral. Joivan Wade recommends having at least five people, ideally with larger followings than you, or around your audience size, with whom you can regularly exchange likes and comments.

One method I have found a tremendous amount of success with is by identifying large pages or networks of large pages that are willing to allow you to advertise on their accounts. The best way to go about this is to identify pages in your niche and direct message them on Instagram asking for their advertising rates. Most of them will come back with what it costs to do a "shout out" or a message of support for your page across their page or network. I always respond and ask them for a guaranteed follower package (e.g., I advertise X number of dollars and you guarantee me X followers in return). Most accounts will respond saying they don't offer this type of package, so you have to find the accounts that are confident enough and willing to offer this type of support; otherwise, a normal shout out will only get you a few hundred followers max. Find the accounts or networks that are creative and really good at driving traffic that results in followers.

In addition, you have to test many of these networks to weed out the ones that will sell you fake/bot followers. The only way to test these networks is by segmenting the tests on different days (i.e., test one network one day and another network another day). I recommend only spending a few hundred dollars with each network first and see who delivers high-quality (real) engaged followers before scaling. Once you find the network that delivers, then you can scale.

Your Network Is Everything

Julius Dein used the tactic of reposting to grow his page. He had pages in the meme niche post his content on their accounts while crediting him. Every time these accounts would post one of his videos, he would get another twenty, thirty, or forty thousand new followers. By using this strategy, he gained up to a hundred thousand followers a week. He says that the key to success on the platform is good content and good distribution. Your network is everything.

Keep in mind, however, that Dein's rapid growth is a bit out of the norm. Massive growth on Instagram usually doesn't happen as quickly as it does on Facebook. Normally, people get 25,000 to 50,000 followers a month, max. This is a far cry from a million followers in thirty days on Facebook. For growth to happen you need to be patient and consistent over time. Of course, if Kim Kardashian likes or comments on your content, massive growth can scale more quickly, but your content needs to be really good, and you have the real challenge of getting her to see it.

To boost your own ability to become influential on the platform, keep in mind that consistency is key. Joivan Wade explains that Instagram's algorithm places you in one of three categories: (A) posting at least twice a day, constantly engaging with comments and likes from your audience, and engaging with other people's posts and commenting (this behavior creates a prime account—most likely to hit the Explore page and influence other pages to hit the Explore page); (B) posting every other day, a few times a week, and only sometimes engaging with user comments and likes; or (C) posting once in a blue moon, never really commenting back to other users' comments, and not engaging in activity with creators. Which one are you currently? Exhibit A-like behavior to be an Instagram superstar.

Choosing Influencers

Since influencers and big accounts can play an important role in driving growth on Instagram, you need to be strategic in choosing whom you collaborate with. Not all influencers will be beneficial to your brand or message. Just because they're popular and have a large following doesn't mean they'll help your visibility.

Test influencers just like you would content. David Oh of FabFitFun says that his team tested more than five thousand influencers before finding the ones who worked best for their brand. He urges you to be diligent—you can't just try one and expect results. Oftentimes the influencers David's team initially hypothesized to be the best weren't always the ones who created the most successful results.

After a lot of trial and error, Oh found that one of the best influencers for FabFitFun is Tori Spelling. She's great at creating compelling content. After seeing how well her videos performed, FabFitFun took them, analyzed what worked, and made a tutorial about how to create similar videos. They passed the tutorials along to their other influencers and now all of them create content in a similar style. Oh has found that supporting his influencers with their own brands has helped his company's reach.

He recalls that in the beginning, building relationships with influencers was a funny process—his team tried all sorts of crazy strategies. Once, someone on his team passed a request to the dentist of the brother of the influencer they were trying to target. Believe it or not, they succeeded, and FabFitFun still works with that influencer to this day. Do what it takes to reach these people (but try not to be too creepy).

Oh's team didn't have a lot of money when they started, so they targeted smaller influencers and, at first, exchanged FabFitFun products for posts. Once they started working with people who were known throughout the influencer network, they found themselves in an influencer bubble—other important influencers started to know them. If you can get a buzz going about your product or brand, often influencers will start coming to you. For example, if a few people on *Dancing with the Stars*, *The Bachelorette*, or *The Real Housewives of Beverly Hills* are interested in your brand, product, or ideas, other reality stars will start to notice you. And if you have something valuable to offer, celebrities will start to want to get it as well.

If you don't have a product, think about what you can offer an influencer. Sometimes an influencer will work with you because of your compelling content. Other times, it's because you can offer them something, like taking pictures of them or featuring them in cool collaborative content. Think about what the influencer may need and how your skill set can enhance theirs.

Influencing the Influencer

Ken Cheng, founder and director at Jengo, a digital marketing and strategy company, has advice for getting celebrities to notice your brand. He doesn't focus on building a huge following on Instagram. Instead, his team focuses on reaching the people who already have that following and lets them do the work of spreading the message for his clients. He explains that it's not about going to the biggest influencers or celebrities directly. You have a much better chance of success if you focus on influencing the influencers who influence your target influencer. (It might sound confusing now, but wait for it . . .) There's a network effect where smaller influencers influence the bigger ones—their content moves upstream and is seen by more influential people. To make this happen, first you need to follow the accounts of the super influencers you're trying to target. Then, look through and discover which micro- or easier-to-reach influencers they follow. Observe the types of posts that the big influencers like on the microinfluencer's accounts. Once you know if the microinfluencer's posts are related to the topics of your brand, and that the bigger influencer is paying attention to those types of posts, you can reach out to the smaller influencer to post about your brand or message.

Adley Stump says that you can go through influencers' posts and see who comments to figure out who is in their engagement circles and to find stronger influencers in your specific niche. Approaching the smaller influencers first is a much more effective strategy than going to the big influencers directly. Eventually you may reach them, but it's smart to work your way up the ladder from smaller influencers to larger ones.

Targeting smaller accounts that fewer people (albeit valuable people) pay attention to has worked for Cheng on many occasions. He once worked with a Vietnamese restaurant in New York that wanted big celebrity attention. Initially, the restaurant tried to contact agents and publicists, but nothing came out of it; it ended up just wasting money for a couple of months. After this experience, it started targeting and having success with influencers with around ten thousand followers, then those with twenty thousand followers, and so on and so forth, until it started getting influencers in the hundred thousand–plus range. It was at this time that celebrities started coming to the restaurant on their own. Even Sarah Jessica Parker ended up coming in and tweeting about the restaurant without any solicitation or pay.

This process happened organically over time by influencing the people around the big celebrity. Sarah Jessica Parker came in because she saw other smaller influencers and friends whom she followed on Instagram posting about a great new restaurant in New York, which encouraged her to make the decision to go and try the food herself.

Tagging and Using Privacy Settings to Gain Followers

Anthony Arron, comedian and founder of Instagram account imjustbait, which gets around a hundred million impressions a week and fifty million views a month, agrees that to get content to go viral, you need to use a circle of influencers. If you're in a network of big pages posting your content, you'll receive more attention. That's what most of the people he knows with big accounts do to gain views and to go viral.

Additionally, Arron has found that playing with the privacy settings of his account is the best way to capture more followers. He posts ten to fifteen videos a day on his page, spreading the posts throughout the day to reach people in different time zones. When he posts a video, he leaves his page on the public account setting so that a lot of new people can see it. However, he's found that even though people see and like the videos, they won't necessarily follow him. To combat this problem, he will randomly set his account to private after he posts the videos to encourage people to follow him to access the locked content.

Sometimes he'll have upward of eighty thousand people watching a video and tagging their friends to view it as well. When people's friends come to watch the video and see that the account is on private, they'll usually follow the page because they want to see the video that their friends have tagged them in. The key is, if the content is good enough, people will follow him for the opportunity to see it. This forces him to keep creating good content so these people won't later unfollow him. This strategy has brought Arron around two thousand to five thousand followers a day.

He also puts a watermark on all his videos that says, "Follow @imjustbait." That way, whether people repost, save, or simply view his videos, they're more likely to know about his account and follow him.

Erick Brownstein of Shareability agrees that getting people to tag their friends in posts is a great strategy. Since Instagram is not as shareable a type of platform as Facebook, his team finds that tagging is the best way to help people spread content. Tagging is like a personal invitation to get someone to see something. It's the way people show their friends content they think will be relevant to their tastes.

Good Content
for Lasting Growth

Ray Chan, CEO and cofounder of 9GAG, an online platform for humor with over forty-one million followers on Instagram, has learned a lot about achieving massive growth on the platform. He suggests using other platforms, if you have them, to drive people to Instagram. Then he suggests comparing your account to the best accounts in your niche and getting ideas from them. Chan also explains that his team is continuously testing different hashtags and post formats.

For example, a current video-formatting trend people use to stand out is having big captions at the top of videos to catch people's short attention spans. This originated on motivational posts with black frames at the top and the picture below. But these trends change, and you shouldn't rely too heavily upon them. You always need to listen to your user by way of monitoring your analytics.

Chan recommends that instead of searching for growth hacks, you should focus on creating great content and a great community. He uses the stock market as a metaphor. Many people try to get rich quick, or in this case build a bunch of followers too quickly, which is not a good long-term strategy. Building up a solid platform over time is like picking a good stock and holding on to it for a while.

What often happens is people look for quick tips to grow their accounts, which is like trying to pick a stock that will quickly rise. But great investors don't look at the short term; they try to find stocks that will rise consistently over time. And that's what Chan's team tries to do. They still have to learn the tricks and understand the latest trends and formats, but you never know whether a trend will have long-term benefits until you test it over time.

To have growth on Instagram you have to constantly stay up-to-date. The core principle is thinking about what your users want to see. Creating good content that your user likes is the not-so-secret secret sauce.

Chan's team has two personalities when they create content. On the one hand, they use empathy to figure out why certain content works in the eyes of their viewers. And on the other hand, they become very detached from the content to create distance and space, which allows them to make changes to content that doesn't work. Chan notices that many people get too attached to their content, which prevents them from testing and learning to see what their viewers want and how people respond. It's the difference between being an artist and being a commercial artist. He feels that Andy Warhol was an example of someone who was both. If you want to be commercially successful, you probably have to be willing to change a little bit of what you're creating and keep your users in mind.

Joivan Wade adds that you don't have to guess what your users like. If you have a business profile, you can use the insights page to see your most viewed posts in the last year. This helps you understand which content your users are actively engaging with and allows you to create more content of this nature.

Don't Have a Hidden Agenda

Chan feels that one reason Instagram, and social media in general, can be hard for some people to master is because they approach it with a hidden agenda. The common thread of the top accounts on Instagram is that their content is really engaging. They don't ask you to do anything outside the normal habit of a user that browses Instagram.

One of the top accounts, for example, is National Geographic. It's successful because obviously it's very visual, and also because its content is its end goal. It doesn't ask anyone to go out and buy or watch something else. People go to the page to see beautiful photos and watch great videos. Viewers might want to buy the magazine and watch the shows as a result, but this is never pushed on the platform.

Great content is what makes people want to follow a page, not your desire as a creator to get someone to follow you. You have to do what's best for the followers, not what's best for your agenda. Create the highest-quality content and the best experience for the people you're trying to reach. Through that, you'll foster stronger connections and build a more solid community.

At the core, Chan thinks people want to be surprised and to feel happier after seeing content. Understand the fundamentals of storytelling; be a great storyteller and figure out the real psychological principles behind great storytelling. Then make sure that you're leveraging those strategies in the content you create. Make sure people understand what you're telling them and test the formats that are most effective for your content.

Instant Consumption

Although the content rules you learned in chapter five apply to all the platforms, there are some differences when it comes to the format in which you present content on Instagram. First of all, Brownstein says that one way to think of Instagram is as the fifty-nine-second version of the content you create. Wade agrees and advises using Instagram to drive people to other platforms to see the content in its longer format.

Chan contributes that the time spent on Instagram for each piece of content is very short. Most people who browse Instagram are looking for very instant consumption. They don't want to spend as much time with the content as they do on other platforms. They just have a look at it, notice that it's pretty or funny, like it, and move on to the next picture or video. This requires your content on Instagram to be more colorful. It needs to be different and catch people's attention.

Observe Other Accounts

Chan also explains that a great way to start out with Instagram content creation is to find accounts or brands that have similar goals and that are achieving a lot of success. Then, find similar formats and structures but don't necessarily copy them. Try to be innovative, even if you're only making slight changes because, Chan emphasizes, "copying other peoples' content is like creating a body without a soul." He recommends moving your captions on the pictures to different areas; creating titles with typos so people will try to correct you and comment; and doing remixes of old types of formats you see on the platform. Discover whether you can create a new remix or adapt an old one.

Use Behind-the-Scenes Moments

Tim Greenberg of the World Surf League says that Instagram has been great for business. The World Surf League tend to showcase younger surfers' footage because its audience is younger on this platform. And it shares more funny moments in real time through Instagram stories than on Facebook. Sometimes content on both platforms is duplicated, but usually on Instagram it features more behind-the-scenes moments of the athletes letting their guard down.

For example, the page put up a video of Brazilian professional surfer Gabriel Medina kicking a soccer ball around that created massive engagement with more than three hundred thousand views. The World Surf League specifically choose not to put that video on Facebook or any other platform because it felt more like Instagram material—more *in the moment* and visceral.

Medina is one of the most followed surfers on Instagram and does a great job of telling stories. Greenberg also cites Hawaiian professional surfer Coco Ho as someone who does an incredible job of building her brand online. And as such, she has generated a lot of sponsorship dollars. They both stand out as consistent producers of great content on Instagram.

Greenberg tells all his athletes that a video of them waxing their board might seem monotonous in their eyes, but to someone in Kansas it's interesting because it portrays a lifestyle and a dream that others may never experience. Or, if a surfer is on Tavarua in Fiji enjoying a Ping-Pong game with their buddies, it might be normal to them, but it's probably really interesting to their followers. It took a long time for his athletes to understand that, but now they're getting really good at gauging what content to share.

A lot of the content that the World Surf League produces is user generated. Although it self-produces content and runs events, it leans on a network of videographers and photographers around the globe to provide material. The league generates a lot of its engagement because of its network of contributors. It's really important to remember that you don't have to create everything yourself. You can lean on people in your community to help you.

How to Approach
Instagram for a Local Market

Ken Cheng of Jengo explains that Instagram is a great tool for local businesses. One reason is that, unlike some of the other platforms that rely on broad-scope content (which has nothing to do with a person's life outside the digital world), the use of Instagram stems from experiences that originate off-line. Instagram users want to go places for the opportunity to take and share photos on the platform. Thus, the release of a product can become an experience to document—it can bring people to a restaurant or a clothing store so they have the opportunity to share the story of interacting with a local business.

Once Cheng's team realized the way the platform worked, the challenge was driving traffic to their clients' accounts. When they began, they had a limited budget, which made it hard to build traffic in a short period. As a result, they decided to leverage other influencers' traffic. The next challenge was figuring out which influencers to target. They were promoting restaurants and although you can use the typical hashtag search to find people in the restaurant and food space, it's difficult to search for influencers in a specific category. However, now there are websites such as FameBit, Social Native, and Grapevine that you can use to help you with this process.

For example, they wanted to find influencers featuring Asian noodles in New York. But it's hard to tell if an influencer is local. You can go through their photos and find their geotags, but if you don't have a list of influencers to start with, Instagram isn't very supportive in reaching that goal.

To identify if your influencer's followers are local, you can either manually look through their followers or search for a program that helps you. When choosing a good influencer for your local brand, make sure that person lives in your area and will post about your specific topic; 40 to 60 percent of an influencer's regular posts and 15 to 35 percent of viral posts should be geared toward and received by your specific geo-targeted audience. If the influencer lives in your area but most of their followers don't, it won't help your objective.

The next step depends on how much money you have to spend, but Cheng shares that he doesn't typically pay influencers. To get influencers in the most cost-efficient manner, his company uses free food in exchange for an influencer's visit. Also, they never directly ask influencers to post photos about them. They always just say, "We saw your photos and they're amazing!" Talk about their photos and invite them to dinner in your restaurant or to an event at your local business. Provide them with value instead of just trying to sell them something.

His team also discovered that people with more than a hundred thousand followers usually ignored them if they weren't compensated economically. For no pay, typically someone in the ten to twenty thousand follower range was more likely to show interest. Besides, the larger their influence, the more global the traffic. A more micro-influencer with a ten-thousand-person following could actually be a better fit for your local business. Also, people with fewer followers actually need the content and appreciate it more. After they built relationships with smaller influencers, they started to reach out to ones in the forty to fifty thousand person range, then the sixty to seventy thousand range, and so on and so forth.

Don't forget to think from the influencers' point of view and offer them value. Give them something they already need, want, or are using. To be effective in this regard, refer back to some of the strategies we offered for building partnerships in chapter six.

Quick Tips and Recap

- Growth is slower on Instagram than on Facebook. Be patient and consistent over time. Gaining twenty-five thousand to thirty thousand followers a month is a lot.

- Your network is everything. Find engagement groups and people selling power likes. There are also a ton of Facebook groups that offer shout-out for shout-outs (s4s) and engagement group opportunities.

- Use the Explore page to get discovered.

- Get high-profile accounts (those with a larger number of followers and those who have been on the platform for a long time) to like, comment, mention you, and repurpose your content.

- Encourage people to tag you in your posts. Even incentivize them with a follow back.

- The caption is everything when it comes to naturally encouraging engagement.

- If you are a brand, use visual and behind-the-scenes moments on this platform.

- Target smaller influencers first and work your way up.
- Currently time spent with an individual piece of content on Instagram is very short. Although with the launch of IGTV, IG is trying to change that behavior.
- Let your content be the end goal.
- Use the platform to help you attract influencers that influence your target influencer.
- Instagram can be of great use to local businesses because of the off-line experiences it promotes.

CHAPTER 9

GROWTH DRIVERS FOR YOUTUBE

Y ouTube is one of the hardest platforms on which to grow quickly and on which to go viral. Similar to Instagram, it's not set up as an inherently shareable platform. Similar to SEO, the goal is to rank well enough within YouTube's algorithms to get your content filtered to the top of search results and to be included in suggested viewing.

Jackie Koppell, principal on-camera talent and creator at NewsyNews and recently chosen by YouTube for the inaugural Women in Comedy program, is also the former head of talent at AwesomenessTV, a multiplatform media company. Koppell explains that twenty thousand subscribers is the minimum amount you need to get the algorithms to pay attention to you, fifty thousand sub-scribers to start making money, and a hundred thousand subscribers to get brands to pay attention to you.

She says that one strategy for growth is to leverage the viral and rapid growth potential of Facebook to build a large audience and then drive those fans to follow your YouTube channel. As we have discussed in earlier chapters, advertising dollars go much further on the Facebook platform than on YouTube's advertising platform— they're a lot cheaper and you can achieve faster growth. Once you establish rapid growth on Facebook, it becomes easier to push people to your YouTube channel. Beyond that strategy, there are other growth and efficiency tactics you can apply on the YouTube platform itself.

Watch Time Is King

With YouTube's algorithms, watch time is king, so the percentage of time that people watch your videos is more important than how many people view them. Success is contingent upon creating great, high-quality content that people want to watch for a long time and upon utilizing strategic collaborations that help you grow.

Unlike on any of the other platforms, longer content does really well on YouTube. Joivan Wade, founder of "The Wall of Comedy!" explains that people will actually come to the platform to watch long pieces of content. An eight-minute video seems like an optimal amount of time and will be very well received (if it's good).

Erick Brownstein of Shareability says that his team thinks You-Tube is particularly valuable for the long haul because content lives there forever and is easily searchable. If your content is solid, it can get picked up in other places as well and you can start to build organically.

Content Discovery and Growth

Brownstein explains that people typically discover content in three ways: (1) Everyone starts sharing your content and it goes viral—the best way, but extremely hard to make happen on YouTube since it's not an inherently shareable platform. (2) Through search. If you hit metadata and trends that people are already searching, it's a great way to get discovered. (3) Through other people's content, which is a big reason collaborations come in handy.

Jonathan Skogmo, CEO of Jukin Media and creator of the You-Tube channel FailArmy, with more than thirteen million subscribers, has had major success. In fact, when "Gangnam Style" was the number one most watched video in the world, Skogmo's company had the second most watched video, "The Ultimate Girls Fail Compilation 2012."[1] "Gangnam Style" had four hundred million views in November 2012, and "Ultimate Girls Fail" had 290 million. Skogmo shares that his company has seen YouTube make all sorts of changes in their algorithms based on users' behaviors and reactions. If you're a content creator, you must be agile enough to make quick changes and tweaks as YouTube changes. Study the platform and continuously pay attention to what does well. This goes back to the idea of testing and learning, although being searchable is always going to be one of the keys to growth.

Chris Williams, the founder and CEO of pocket.watch and former chief audience officer of Maker Studios, where he oversaw

---

[1] "The Ultimate Girls Fail Compilation 2012," YouTube video, 10:14, posted by FailArmy, November 22, 2012, https://www.youtube.com/watch?v=Gng3sPiJdzA.

more than sixty thousand channels, says that the best way to grow on YouTube is a combination of paid media, collaborations, optimizations, and playlisting. He's a big believer in using paid media to lead to organic growth. He adds that follow-on views—the amount of content people watch after the initial video they're driven to—is the truest indication of organic growth coming off paid media expenses.

He uses AdSense to track which videos his viewers watch. His team determines the effectiveness of a piece of content by how much more content it gets people to consume. This indicator dictates their strategy and influences how his team uses paid media to fuel growth. It gives them insight into both the content and the marketing strategy.

Jackie Koppell adds that she has seen people grow quickly with giveaways. When she was at AwesomenessTV she saw people give away fancy cameras or iPads. If you can do that consistently (which she realizes most people can't) your numbers start to skyrocket.

Collaborations Lead to Quick Organic Growth

One of the best ways to build a community on YouTube is through collaborations with other YouTubers. Sharing audiences isn't a novel concept—it's something that people have been talking about for the last ten years—but it really does work. Your collaborators' biggest fans will subscribe to everyone in the collaboration group.

Phil Ranta, the former COO of Studio71, one of the largest influencer-driven digital entertainment companies, has used strategic partnerships to grow YouTube influencers' followings. His team has done a lot of work with Rhett & Link (4.4 million subscribers), who collaborate with TV host Jimmy Fallon.

Rhett & Link created "Good Mythical Morning," a YouTube talk show. Rhett & Link and Fallon's shows have similar styles but reach different audiences. Fallon has an older, more traditional fan base, and Rhett & Link have a younger, scrappier fan base. To collaborate and share audiences, they started appearing on each other's shows. Fallon does episodes of "Good Mythical Morning," and Rhett & Link make appearances on *The Tonight Show*. It has been really advantageous for both parties. Working with Fallon has brought Rhett & Link to the mainstream, while at the same time has helped Fallon break into the digital world.

Collaborations also work well for people who are just starting. Ranta has seen people start out time and again with only ten subscribers and then generate more than two hundred thousand new fans a week through collaborations. Growth from optimal collaborations can happen swiftly on YouTube. For example, Ranta was running channel partnerships at Fullscreen when YouTube personality Shane Dawson was in the network. During this time, he observed that Dawson was an expert collaborator who could launch careers. He watched Dawson take smaller creators under his wing and collaborate with them in a bunch of videos; oftentimes they'd become huge stars even before they started posting their own videos aggressively. Dawson's collaborations have helped internet personalities like Shanna Malcolm and Alexis G. Zall increase their fandom.

Remember what we learned about collaborating from the Instagram chapter—when starting out, you don't have to collaborate with someone of Shane Dawson's size. Even if the person you collaborate with only has ten thousand subscribers, there's a chance that three hundred of their fans will start following your channel. And if you have zero to a hundred subscribers, start collaborating with someone who has a thousand. Work your way up the ladder.

Chris Williams agrees that strategic partnerships and collaborations are vital for scale and growth. His team feels that they're an extraordinarily efficient means of creating a "conference of cool." Essentially, they allow the audience to find and like you because you're associated with something they already gravitate toward. Collaborations drive a direct audience in a fairly efficient way.

Additionally, Ranta has noticed that a lot of YouTubers move to the same apartment complexes in L.A. to make it easier to collaborate. Apparently, a lot of the top social influencers have lived in the Hollywood and Vine building at some point (tough luck for the neighbors who aren't YouTubers).

However, Koppell points out that you don't want to prematurely move to L.A. just for this reason. Exhaust the connections that you can make from your hometown first. And if you have at least ten thousand subscribers, you can film at the YouTube offices in major cities all over the world, including Los Angeles, New York, Paris, and London,[2] one day a month free of charge, which is a great way to make connections and start meeting people. Do as much networking as you can before moving so the transition is easier if and when you do decide to move.

Focus Your Efforts and Frequency

Ranta believes that to build a solid audience on YouTube, you should focus most of your efforts on the content creation for that channel. He doesn't suggest that you ignore other platforms while building an audience on YouTube but says that you're better off making five

---

[2] YouTube Space, https://www.youtube.com/yt/space.

YouTube videos rather than two YouTube videos, two Facebook posts, and a podcast. He explains that size begets growth, so an optimal strategy is to make the bulk of the content on YouTube and then use the other social platforms to engage with fans and promote YouTube video views. When people put their main effort into YouTube, he sees them get more total subscribers than when they try to build everything at once.

Also, if you create good YouTube content daily, it's amazing for your growth. Ranta says that the fastest way to grow is to take more swings, and the way to take more swings is to make more videos. Frequency is really important for building an audience, especially when you're starting out. Of course, you shouldn't put up content you don't like, but if you're a vlogger and only post once a week, it's really hard to keep up with people who post every day. Fans are there every day, so if you vlog four times in a row and then you're not there for a few days, people will start forgetting about you.

Have a Strong Point of View and Stick to One Theme

Ranta believes the number one thing that every successful YouTube creator has in common is a strong point of view around which they consistently create content. Their point of view could be related to their comedic sense of humor, makeup style, or fitness ideas, but they have to have something that makes them unique.

Once you recognize what sets you apart, highlight that attribute or theme on your channel. If you keep at it, you'll usually find success. This is more important than looking good on camera or having a lot of experience as a vlogger. Ranta has observed that even those with great skill usually don't achieve success if they don't stick to one topic. Changing topics too often becomes very confusing for people. Approach your content from a single point of view and you'll have a better chance of finding your audience.

When you review YouTube comments, you'll see that the videos and channels people love most are ones that make them feel like they're connecting with their best friends. It's really hard to feel like someone is your best friend if you can't explain what they're about. Keep it simple and start with a narrow focus.

Two-Way Conversations

YouTube offers people a community and a place to go and speak with others. One of the biggest differences between the success of social stars and traditional movie or television stars is that the social content creator is perceived like they're talking to their friends, while the movie or television star is more distant. A social star is inspirational, while a movie star is aspirational.

Ranta explains that when you're a vlogger or a personality, there's a preexisting expectation that the audience is watching someone who could potentially be their friend or interact with them. The audience loves the idea that they can be mentioned in a comment. Some reasonably big creators do have one-way conversations—like basic how-tos or Vivo channels. However, those work because they're enjoyed more like television, where comments are less important. But if your goal is to be a YouTube personality or a host, then the two-way conversation is vital. You should be talking to your audience, making them feel included as if they're your friends.

Passion and Knowledge

Ranta shares that you're doing the wrong thing if you don't love what you're talking about. People who succeed on this platform are extremely passionate about the topics of their videos. And since there's such an open market, there's an audience for almost everything, as long as you're creating cool content.

There are some deep cultures online. For example, if you're into superheroes or comic books, there are a lot of fanatics out there. You must really know what you're talking about to make a channel like that work. Ranta explains that if you're someone who goes home and thinks, "Marvel stuff is popular. I'll be a Marvel commentator," but you're not actually an expert, people will smell your inauthenticity immediately and the content will flop.

Make sure that you're knowledgeable and passionate about the topic you discuss on your channel. This authentic passion is what people respond positively toward. Plus, you'll enjoy learning everything about something you love. It will help you stay motivated and give you fuel to put in the necessary effort to create a channel that thrives.

Be the Same but Different

To start generating an audience on YouTube, you need to follow the basic content patterns and trends. You usually can't come out of nowhere with content that's totally unfamiliar. The biggest thing Ranta always tells people is to *be the same but different*. Your style needs to be recognizable and people need to understand what's going on, but it needs to be distinct enough that someone will follow you over another vlogger.

Koppell points out that makeup tutorials and gaming channels do really well, and family/kid content is the reigning champion on YouTube. She also explains that a current popular trend to generate more watch time on your channel is to use cues that encourage people to stay. You can say things like, "I can't wait to tell you guys—I'm gonna reveal my secret surprise at the end of the video." Or if you're doing a beauty tutorial, you can say, "Stay till the end of the video, guys, because I'm gonna reveal the entire look."

Although you should follow the tips mentioned above, you also need to develop your own unique way of doing things. Find your authentic voice and formula. Make sure to bring your distinctive personality and show people who you truly are. There is no one like you and if you bring your whole self to the camera, it will help you shine and gain more fans.

Viral Machines

Ranta's company, Studio71, works with Roman Atwood, one of the top social influencers in the world, with more than fourteen million subscribers, who has created viral videos that have received more than 4.5 billion views. Atwood rose to fame from doing viral prank videos and then used that success to create a daily vlog that was more family friendly.

Atwood is a viral machine. He hasn't just had virals here and there but has had consistent viral videos. A lot of that is because he understands pacing and what makes something clickable or entertaining. He didn't have to go to acting class or hosting school. Once

Atwood started doing pranks online, he just had a way with the camera, and he is good looking, young, and energetic.

Ranta explains that he read an interesting article about Michael Phelps and why he's such a successful swimmer. Apparently, Phelps was born with an enlarged heart and had noticeably webbed fingers—it's as though he were born to be a swimmer. Ranta feels that many YouTube stars are famous for the same reasons—it's as if they were engineered in a lab to be perfect YouTubers. Ranta says that the people who do well listen and learn. They absorb information when it comes to optimization and programming strategy. And they observe their fans' behavior and cater to it.

Chris Williams agrees that personality is a big indicator of how successful one will be on YouTube. But to do further analysis, his team studied Ryan ToysReview, the largest YouTube creator channel in the world and also a partner of Chris's company, to try and determine some of the attributes that led to the channel's phenomenal growth. According to Forbes, this year alone the six-year-old host, Ryan, has made $11 million in revenue from his YouTube account. The channel was tied for eighth on Forbes' annual list of the highest-earning YouTube accounts.[3] (Quite a lucky kid, since he gets to live many children's dreams of getting paid to play with and review toys on the channel.)

Williams feels that much of Ryan's success is because he appears multicultural. This concept was brought to his attention while watching an interview with Dwayne "the Rock" Johnson, where he was

---

[3] John Lynch, "A 6-Year-Old Boy Is Making $11 Million a Year on YouTube Reviewing Toys," *Business Insider*, December 8, 2017, https://flipboard.com/@flipboard/-a-6-year-old-boy-is-making-11-million-a/f-3ff3f0cd46%2Fbusinessinsider.com.

asked about his popularity. The Rock explained that he thinks that many people resonate with him because they believe they share his nationality and ethnicity. They think the Rock "is their thing" because he relates to a lot of different ethnic communities. Williams says that Ryan has a similar appeal. He sees that being perceived as multicultural is a rewarding attribute on YouTube. He also thinks that Ryan's mom's infectious laugh (as she is the one who holds the camera) has contributed to the channel's success. And, of course, the selection of content and toys that Ryan reviews contribute to his success.

Koppell adds that the greatest influencers work hard. As easy as it is for people to diminish what influencers do, the reality is they are good at what they do—there's something about them that people want to watch. They consistently put up content and put themselves out there adapting with the times. She finds this respectable and valuable.

Value in Multichannel Networks

Multichannel networks (MCNs) collaborate with video platforms like YouTube to offer assistance to channel owners in areas like digital rights management, programming, funding, partner management, audience development, product, cross promotion, monetization, or sales in exchange for some of the channel's advertising revenue.

The decision to join a network on YouTube is based on where you are in your career and where you want to go. MCNs can be extremely helpful, but they're like signing with any agent or manager—you don't want to be at the bottom of anyone's roster. You don't want to be in a one-size-fits-all situation that doesn't suit your brand's needs.

For example, Ranta explains that if an MCN offers you access to a tech platform where you'll get deep data and analytics, you can make better decisions, but if you're not overinterested in deciphering data and analytics, it's probably not the right MCN for you. However, if you're ready to package and sell your own television show, and it's an MCN that has a track record of success in that area, perhaps pursuing it could be highly valuable.

Reaching Kids and Analyzing Metrics

Williams shares that if your audience demographic is kids and families, YouTube is great because it's "where kids live." Over 70 percent of children's video content consumption is done on streaming platforms. And YouTube dominates in terms of watch time with kids. It's been his company's primary platform for growth as they cater to this demographic.

When working with kids, your metrics are not related entirely to the number of subscribers you gain, since children are too young to subscribe. Instead, his team focuses on the strategy of optimizing for algorithms that allow them prominent placement inside suggested and related videos. They usually pay attention to metrics like watch time and follow-on views (how many other videos a viewer views after the initial video) to judge the effectiveness of their tactics.

Going Viral

Filmmaker and CEO/creative director at Comp-A Productions, Pedro D. Flores, who personally has more than 239,000 subscribers and the viral hit "Tacos" has over 100 million views, explains that going viral is always a roll of the dice. You can put in all the right recipes for the perfect viral video, but you honestly never know if it's going to be successful.

He never thought that the parody video "Tacos," about the fact that he is a non-Mexican-looking Mexican, would go viral. That success changed his whole perspective on the type of content he wanted to create. Before that video, he had never made anything about his ethnicity. But after seeing how well the audience responded, he now caters to that niche. You won't start out knowing what works for you. You will discover your viewers' tastes by creating content, testing, and learning—sound familiar?

Flores says that you have to constantly shift. And he would know. Flores has been on the YouTube platform since the very beginning. He created early viral sensations "Kings of Myspace" and "Kings of YouTube" (you will actually find me in this video if you look hard enough). He was also the director and frequent collaborator of a lot of YouTube stars, such as Timothy DeLaGhetto (3.6 million subscribers) and SUPEReeeGo's Eric Ochoa (2.8 million subscribers). He's also successfully transferred his channel from having content only in English to being a channel with all content in Spanish. Then he shifted from a Spanish channel using real people to one using mostly cartoons. You have to be willing to change with the times and go with the trends. He says that if you don't keep up, you will get left behind.

Quick Tips and Recap

- On YouTube you need to have at least twenty thousand subscribers for algorithms to respond, fifty thousand subscribers to start making money, and a hundred thousand subscribers to get brands to pay attention.

- Currently, YouTube's algorithms favor content with a high percentage of watch time. Longer content does well on YouTube.

- YouTube is one of the most difficult platforms on which to achieve rapid growth.

- Growth happens primarily through algorithms, search, and collaborations.

- Be consistent and put out content daily.

- Collaboration is key to rapid growth on YouTube.

- Move to Hollywood and Vine to find YouTube collaborators. Just kidding (sort of).

- If you have ten thousand subscribers, you can film at the YouTube offices one day a month, free of charge.

- Determine the effectiveness of a piece of content by how much more content it gets people to consume.

- Use AdSense to track which videos people view.

- Analyze your metrics by way of subscribers, watch time, and follow-on views depending on your needs.

- Have a strong point of view in your content and on your channel.

- Stick to one topic or viewpoint on your channel.

- If your goal is to be a personality or a host, then the two-way conversation with your fans is important.

- Be passionate and knowledgeable about your topic.
- Be the same but different in your approach to topics and content creation style.
- Makeup tutorials, gaming channels, and family-friendly programs reign supreme on YouTube.
- Use cues to encourage people to stay and watch your content.
- Feature your fans in your vlogs to gain their interest.
- Work hard, be flexible, and adapt as the platform changes.

CHAPTER 10

THE REALITIES OF SNAPCHAT

T his chapter is going to be short. I'm choosing to keep it that way for the same reason I haven't included a chapter on Twitter: I don't use these platforms. I don't see them giving people the opportunities for growth and monetization the way the other platforms do. In fact, as you'll learn in this chapter, many Snapchat influencers are leaving and moving over to Instagram Stories. A lot of the content strategies you'll learn here can also be applied to that feature on the Instagram platform. With that said, some brands still find a lot of benefit in using the platform, and there are influencers who have made up to $100,000 a week.

The biggest hurdle to having success on Snapchat is the fact that the only way to grow is either to do collaborations or pay someone popular to do shout-outs. It's extremely hard to get discovered on this platform. There are hardly any search tools and Snapchat made a decision early on not to support influencers.

However, this doesn't mean that there aren't marketing benefits. Christy Choi, CEO of First Influence, a digital marketing company with a core focus on Snapchat, has learned how to use Snapchat as a direct-response vehicle and has seen a lot of success in getting viewers to install her clients' apps. Choi believes that this has worked because of the relationship people have with influencers on the platform. Snapchat is a chatting platform. It's not really about the public display of photos; it's built for a more intimate relationship, where even if the influencer doesn't respond, viewers still feel like they're having a direct line of communication with the person to whom they send the message. This level of intimacy on the platform makes people feel as though they're receiving a personal recommendation when an influencer gives them a call to action. It's like a friend holding your hand and saying, "Hey, check this out. This is really cool."

Content Production and Strategy for Snapchat

Snapchat content works well when it's collaborative and features the audience in some way. While growing various brands' Snapchat accounts, Choi discovered that one successful tactic is to do a weekly participatory story where she gets her audience to respond to questions. For example, she'd create a story around guessing the name of a song or something similar. She'd post the song and the audience would submit their responses. They'd send her either an answer or a selfie with an answer. This was very popular and created high engagement.

Due to Snapchat's collaborative nature, response rates are usually higher than on most other platforms. Because of this, Choi recommends using a call to action and getting people to send you their thoughts or input. Again, people want to feel like they're chatting directly with the influencer, not like they are passively liking or commenting on a post.

Be Authentic

Chris Carmichael, one of the original creators and influencers on Snapchat (the first to build a following of a hundred thousand people) and current CEO of Bitsmash—an app that makes it super easy for anyone to make creative vlogs using just their smartphones—shares his story of becoming popular on this platform. When Snapchat was just starting to become popular in 2014, he was on a trip in Iceland. The platform wasn't really popular in the States yet, but he noticed that in Iceland even grandparents were using snaps as a communication tool. By observing this behavior, his intuition told him that the platform was going to take off and he started telling stories every day. On that trip alone, he built up ten thousand views on his snaps. At the time, no one was even thinking of using the platform as an influencer tool, so to have ten thousand views was a novel concept.

Shortly after this success, he moved to New York and collaborated with a bunch of Viners (from the Vine app) to try to help them grow on Snapchat. Eventually, Carmichael built up around 150,000 views a snap and was getting shout-outs from influencers like Jerome Jarre, King Bach, and Vitaly. The conversion rates on those shout-outs were about 10 percent, which is unheard of—usually you only convert around 1 to 2 percent of viewers.

Brands started reaching out to him. Carmichael went from eating ramen noodles to making $10,000 a story for brands like Disney, Universal, Lionsgate, and Fox. He quickly learned that vertical videos (the kind featured on Snapchat and Instagram Stories) were going to be the next medium kids were addicted to. And it was obvious to him that brands had no idea how to use the vertical video medium. A lot of brands were trying to apply the traditional advertising ideology to a platform that just doesn't buy into it. When millennials see a traditional commercial, they're instantly turned off, and since most Snapchat users are between thirteen and thirty-four years old, they immediately smell the inauthenticity. Brands came to Snapchat trying to apply traditional methodologies to a platform that's super intimate, where you can't lie. You can't say things like, "Buy this toothpaste 'cause it will make your life happier." If you lie or try to sell something, you lose your audience. You must be authentic and tell the truth. Also, on vertical videos your facial expressions are very close up—you're right in your audience's face, so if the person speaking is not genuinely in love with the featured product, it's obvious and can work against the brand.

Carmichael notes that a lot of brands also make the mistake of trying to create high-end, polished content for Snapchat, which is not what kids like—they don't relate to that. They relate to messy drawings and mistakes. Choi adds that people don't think about their snaps in advance. They see something, pull out the phone, document, and send; that's the nature of the platform.

Choi brings up Mike Khoury, who gets two hundred thousand views on a single snap on Snapchat, which is a lot for someone who doesn't have a prominent YouTube channel or previous Vine following. He creates comedic content where he rants about things right in the moment. He constantly makes mistakes in his speech, but it works because it's funny and authentic. That's what people on this platform like; it's what gets them to share the Snapchat story.

Kids want to see a real human being, flaws and all. Be authentic, real, and vulnerable with the audience.

Good for Events

Tim Greenberg, chief community officer at the World Surf League, explains that when Instagram Stories started, his team looked at their platforms and said, "Well, we don't want to produce the same content on both platforms, so how do we take a different voice and approach to Snapchat?" They decided that Snapchat would be a way for their fans to follow their social team's journey around the globe, and that Instagram Stories would be reserved for content about the athletes because that's where they get the highest engagement.

The World Surf League sees success with Snapchat when they cover live events like the Billabong Pipe Masters. On this platform, they try to be funnier and more personable. Tim shares that you can have a lot more fun because the content will disappear in twenty-four hours. It's a behind-the-scenes tool for bringing fans closer to the beach. They also try to make it feel as if a friend is talking to you, like, "Hey, I'm at this event. I'm telling this story."

Joivan Wade, founder of "The Wall of Comedy!" adds that you can use the disappearing factor to your advantage. On Snapchat his team will create a piece of content that encourages people to be there at five o'clock on Friday because once five o'clock on Saturday rolls around, that piece of content is gone. They create content that's compelling for the live format—that demands someone to watch it right there and then.

Hard to Get Discovered on the Platform

Choi explains that it's really hard for creators to get discovered on Snapchat. She feels that influencers give platforms "a little extra twinkle" and unfortunately Snapchat has not encouraged their growth on the platform. Recently, the platform has started doing verified check marks for brands/celebrities, and you can also search interests like music. However, when you search interests, they just suggest the top ten musicians, which isn't enough—it doesn't help smaller people grow. The whole user experience just isn't pleasant; Choi says that you feel like you're "digging through a junk box" to find the content you're looking for.

The only way to grow on this platform is by doing shout-outs with fellow influencers. You have to be in each other's stories, share Snapcodes, and follow each other. It's the only way to grow—unless you're already famous like Kylie Jenner, and then of course followers come naturally.

Leverage Collaborations

Carmichael says that to forge relationships, you have to climb the ladder. Meet people at the bottom, get close to them, and get shout-outs. Create something unique that no one else does, and if people think you're going to grow they'll collaborate with you. You have to approach the low-hanging fruit (people with fewer followers) and hope that someone will want to make a story with you.

When Choi was growing one brand's account, she got most of the followers from paid influencer shout-outs. But on Snapchat you have to do them in a specific way. You don't have the influencer say, "Hey, there's this really cool channel. It does this and this, go follow it." Instead, you make it appear like you're already friends with the large influencer. She asked the influencer to say, "Hey guys, by the way, go say hi to my friend Christy."

After this initiative, thousands of kids started following her. Kids think, "I don't know who Christy is, but she's friends with this person I like and she told me to say hi to her so I'm gonna do it because it's kinda funny." This helped Choi build a massive following because on Snapchat you have to add the person to be able to send them a message. Then on the days she leveraged the influencer's following, she would create an engaging story that prompted people to stick around. She'd use the tactic of featuring fans on the channel saying things like, "Hey, if you're watching my stories you're going to get featured in front of thousands of people." This incentive tends to be successful.

People Are Leaving Snapchat

From a marketing perspective, Choi sees good conversions on Snapchat. If she has the same influencer do the exact same promotion on Snapchat versus Instagram Stories, she actually sees better conversions on Snapchat. The challenge now, however, is that more and more influencers are leaving the platform.

A lot of people are switching to Instagram Stories because they're not growing on Snapchat. They don't actually know how many followers they have and the number of views they receive tends to go down on certain days, which is discouraging. Choi feels that as there's a certain vanity in being an influencer, not knowing how many followers you actually have or seeing your number of views drop can be a problem.

A lot of Snapchat original creators are trying to break into other platforms. Many of them have also gone to musical.ly now, because if you get featured there, you build a following. Most people using social media are trying to grow and it's really hard to do that on Snapchat.

As far as brands are concerned, Choi notices that recently fewer of them are posting on a regular basis. They seem uninterested, either because their platforms are not growing or because they see Snapchat fading away.

Carmichael adds that it's a lot of work and money for brands to hire people who are good at Snapchat. And if someone is good, they'll often go and start their own platform—they have no reason to create solely for one brand. So brands usually end up using their office's social media managers to post content, which generally ends up being uninteresting or static. Further, it's hard for brands to measure if their activity is doing anything for them. So a lot of brands, like influencers, end up focusing on Instagram Stories and leaving Snapchat.

Carmichael thinks that the main reason why everyone is leaving Snapchat is because right from the get-go the platform made the decision not to work with influencers—in fact, they shunned them. They made it very clear that they wouldn't help them. Vine also made the exact same mistake for years. They lost a lot of people to Facebook and Instagram and then tried to get them back, but it was too late, just as it may be too late for Snapchat.

When Instagram copied Snapchat, all the influencers thought, "OK, why would I promote both my Instagram and my Snapchat when I can just promote my Instagram and get both the stories and the image feed?" Instantly, a lot of influencers had way more views on their Instagram Stories because it actually allows you to grow. You can use hashtags to make your story searchable. If you happen to be the top post in a category, you get a lot of views and people can discover your profile and follow you. With Snapchat, on the other hand, there's literally no way to do that; even if you end up on a public story, people can't reach you or find out who you are or add you.

Vertical Videos Are the Future

Carmichael and Choi both believe the future of social media is in vertical videos. They're starting to see musicians such as Selena Gomez and Maroon 5 do music videos in a vertical video format on platforms like Snapchat. Carmichael thinks that this is where video is heading because it's so personal. He says that the vertical video is almost like a window into another person's world. It's like you're holding their hand or are on a FaceTime call. It provides a level of intimacy and connection that horizontal video doesn't evoke.

Taking it a step further, Instagram Stories now allows you to pin/save certain stories so they can stay on your feed forever, like a YouTube video. Because of this, influencers are starting to make and save entertaining narrative-style video stories. They pin them so that people can watch them later. Choi believes that vertical video comedy skits and art-piece narrative stories will dominate in the years to come.

Quick Tips and Recap

- Snapchat was created as a chatting platform. People enjoy the intimacy of snaps and feel as though they're chatting directly with the influencer.
- Create content that's interactive with your audience. Use a call to action. Feature them in your stories. Get fans to send you their thoughts and input or ask them to respond and answer questions. Because of Snapchat's collaborative nature response rates are usually higher than on most other platforms.
- Be authentic, vulnerable, and real.
- Tell the truth. The app shows your face very close up and people can tell if you're lying. (Don't be a Pinocchio!)
- It's OK and even encouraged to make mistakes in the content you create.
- Be consistent and produce content every day.
- Snapchat is good for covering live events.
- The only way to grow on Snapchat is by doing shout-outs and collaborating with fellow influencers. Be in each other's stories, share Snapcodes, and follow each other.
- The only number that matters is how many people see your story per day, not follower numbers like other platforms.

- Because it's so hard to grow on Snapchat, many people are switching over to Instagram Stories.
- Vertical video comedy skits and art-piece narrative stories may be the future of social media.

CHAPTER 11

SUBSTANTIAL BUSINESS GROWTH WITH LINKEDIN

LinkedIn is a powerful platform that can help you target and reach specific people that can lead to significant growth for your business. At first glance, some people just see it as a job-searching and position-filling platform, but if leveraged properly, it can be tremendous for advertising to sell products, strike big deals, and forge career-changing connections. If you have a product, for example, that's beneficial to chief marketing officers (CMOs) of companies with at least a thousand employees, LinkedIn is by far the best and perhaps the only tool that allows you to find those people at scale.

AJ Wilcox, a LinkedIn ad consultant, founded B2Linked.com in 2014, which has managed more than a hundred LinkedIn ad accounts, has spent a cumulative of more than $100 million on the platform (more than any other individual or company worldwide), and has managed three of LinkedIn's top five customers. He believes that LinkedIn is the easiest place to gain access to people who have the job titles, skills, or business-related profile traits you're looking for to build and grow your brand or company.

Biz Development and Forging Strong Partnerships

Wilcox says that LinkedIn is great for searching for jobs because you can connect with anyone you want. Your level of access to people is only limited by your ability to reach out. You can use the search features to find the head of marketing for the company you'd love to work with. If you have a great service for them, nothing stops you from writing a custom connection request saying, "Hey, I've followed you for years and I really love your work. I would love to connect with you." And once you're connected to someone on LinkedIn, you have access to his or her email address or any other profile information they display. You can send emails back and forth for free in an unlimited manner.

If you know someone with whom you'd like to connect—your ideal customer or partner—you can foster a line of communication. The key is to be smart in how you reach out. You don't want to send a request saying, "Hey, I want to get you on the phone and try and sell you something." It's about finding ways to provide value. Start with an initial compliment or something that builds a relationship first without trying to sell anything.

Wilcox points out that everyone hates to be sold to, but everyone loves to buy. So when you first reach out, don't come off like you're there to sell something or it will be the last time you hear from them.

You'll be categorized as spam. I have personally found tremendous success by taking the approach of reaching out with the intent of providing true value to help an individual grow a business or be more successful at work; that can significantly increase the chance of getting a response and can eventually lead to a sale. Don't sell them your service or product; instead offer unique value to them through your product or service. I know this may sound a bit similar, so let me give you an example.

When I was advising a company that was selling social paid optimization (i.e., managing and optimizing social media paid campaigns) for Fortune 100 and 500 companies, I didn't reach out to people and say, "Hi, I would love to talk to you about managing your paid social campaigns. Are you available for a quick call this week?" That is way too salesy and would never get a response. Instead, I would send something along the following lines:

Hi {person's name}, I first want to say congrats on all of your success at {company name}. What you were able to achieve with {cite a specific project, product, or campaign} is truly remarkable.

Because you are an expert in the digital field, I wanted to let you know about a new tech platform we launched that provides exact data on how all of your competitors are spending on social channels, along with insights on their past performance. It also provides deep data on which videos visitors view before and after watching a competitor's video, as well as on which social platforms they viewed the video.

The intriguing part of the platform is all of this data can then be mined and used to increase the quality score of your own videos, which in return drops the cost per view of your own campaigns and increases the organic virality of the video. The best part of the platform is that it is 100 percent transparent and can save you up to {insert impressive statistic} on your paid media campaigns, while also increasing your performance by {insert impressive statistic}.

We are currently working with {list client names} with this new technology. Because you're always on the cutting edge of digital, I wanted to forward the info along as I thought it might be helpful. I would be happy to make an intro to the company if you're interested in learning more.

Best,
Brendan Kane

This message is positioned from the standpoint of providing value to the person to increase the success of their his or her social efforts, not about wanting to sell something. Essentially, you apply the same rules that work for in-person networking. You never walk up to people at a networking event, shove your card in their hand, and say, "Hey, you're from that company. We should do business." That's just going to lead to a lot of people avoiding you on the way to the punch table. Always start with a soft introduction and find out how you can provide value to the other person as quickly as possible.

Content That Generates Leads

Wilcox has had a lot of luck in generating business for his agency by sharing content to stay at the forefront of people's minds. Currently, he has three thousand connections. That number may not seem high, but it's three thousand business connections that all know his value as a LinkedIn specialist who can help them or people they know. If his audience sees him once a month in their feed, or if every time they log in they see something different from him, they'll be more likely to reach out. This is because having people think about you through sharing content allows you to be higher on the call list than other vendors. I can tell you firsthand that this works as I have personally referred several potential clients to AJ.

Wilcox finds the most value in doing simple updates, such as sharing content, thoughts, and experiences once a week rather than using the LinkedIn article feature. This is because no matter what, you're always responsible for driving your own traffic to your content; LinkedIn doesn't do much to help you in that endeavor. But if you have the time and want to write an update about something, of course it can still be helpful. The main point is that leads come from providing free information to people whether you've written the original content or not. As long as the insight is valuable, you're reminding people of your expertise and authority.

You can even share things that are not purely professional. It's totally valid to mix in the personal. For example, Wilcox has seen an HR recruiter write an article about a candidate who came to an interview fifteen minutes late without an apology. The recruiter asked the LinkedIn community if anyone would recommend hiring someone like that. He saw tons of people commenting and saying things like, "No, forget about him," or "Yeah, give him a chance. Maybe he's just an engineer with no social skills." A long conversation happened because of that post.

And this is really valuable because one of the big differences between LinkedIn and other social networks is that any social interaction—a like, a comment, or a share—gets your content seen by a portion of that person's network. If you write something that's compelling enough to get other people to interact with it, you have the opportunity to go viral easily. Your content can reach your network's network, and then that network's network, and so on.

Huge Connection Numbers Don't Necessarily Have a Huge Impact

Wilcox is really selective about his connections on LinkedIn. He'll only connect with someone that he's met in person, or with whom he sees an ability to work. He won't connect to someone just because they're in the same industry. Because of this, he's kept his connection numbers relatively low.

Often he meets people who have fifteen, twenty, or even thirty thousand connections (thirty thousand is the max number of connections that LinkedIn allows, except for people in the extremely exclusive influencer program[1]). But large numbers aren't usually beneficial on LinkedIn due to the fact that when sharing content, it's more advantageous to have a personal connection to the majority of your network. When Wilcox shares something, he has friends and colleagues that actually root for him and cheer him on—they'll like and comment on almost everything he puts out because they're loyal and care about his success. If you have a large audience and no one likes or comments on your content, LinkedIn sees that as less powerful and doesn't show the content to as many people.

---

[1] Tracy Raiteri, "Did You Know That There Are Connection Limits on LinkedIn?" Townsville Social Media Marketing, August 31, 2012, http:// townsvillesocialmediamarketing.com/did-you-know-that-there-are-connection -limits-on-linkedin.

Advertising to
Career-Minded Individuals

LinkedIn is the best place to engage with career-minded individuals. When people are within the LinkedIn ecosystem, they're more business and career focused. They're trying to engage with a business, service, or product, so when you run ads on the platform you're more likely to gain that type of person's attention.

Facebook is a fantastic way of advertising inexpensively, but very few people actually fill in their past and current professional information on their profile. So when you're trying to target people by job titles, you don't have the same scale as you would on LinkedIn. Wilcox notes that on LinkedIn, when you offer someone anything related to work or careers you have insanely high conversion rates, whereas on Facebook you're competing with more content (including photos of people's grandkids and pets, which we all know is more compelling).

Wilcox recommends thinking of LinkedIn ads as sniper targets and of Facebook ads with more of a shotgun approach. You can be much more precise in reaching the business segment of your population with more efficiency on LinkedIn.

Expenses

The attention, level of access, and specificity of targeting you achieve on LinkedIn does come at a high cost, however. Wilcox explains that LinkedIn has one of the most expensive ad platforms out there. On average he sees clicks on LinkedIn cost anywhere between six and nine dollars. Because you're paying a higher amount up front, you need to have a large deal on the back end to make up for the costs.

Before we dive into the ad platform further, I want to say that you can close a lot of business without using the ad platform. Ads are not the only way. For example, I personally closed deals with Disney, Xbox, and Fox, which generated more than $15 million in business simply by messaging the right people with the right message (it cost me nothing). And a good friend of mine closed more than $90 million in business by using the same technique. We actually traded secrets about which messages were performing the best.

Want to know our secret? It's simple—we just try to put ourselves in the other person's shoes and think, "What will make this person's life easier?" Or "What is going to make this guy look like a rock star to his boss?"

However, if you do want to use the ad platform, be sure to pay attention to the list below, since Wilcox gives you the best strategies for how to use the system to your advantage.

Who Should Use the LinkedIn Ad Platform?

There are a few qualifications for the type of people that will benefit most from using the LinkedIn ad platform:

1. Those who have a large deal, meaning they can make $15,000 or more from a deal, a customer, or throughout the lifetime of a client.
2. Those who know the exact type of people who will buy their product. If you think your buyer could be anyone,

LinkedIn isn't the best ad platform for you. It only makes sense when the audience you're targeting is specific and clear—when this is the only place you can reach your customers at scale.

3. White-collar recruiters of almost any type. If your business is trying to hire a sales manager, you can show ads to people in your geo-location whose job title is currently "sales manager" and then every résumé you get will be from a qualified person.

4. Higher education institutions. If you're an MBA school trying to recruit people who have bachelor's degrees but no advanced degrees, and who studied journalism or English, you can hyper target those qualifications to find people who meet those criteria. LinkedIn is the only place where you can do that level of scholastic-related targeting, which makes it great for universities or schools trying to reach new applicants. This is because LinkedIn is one of the only social media platforms where people actually list all their education information. And higher education schools meet the large deal rule because if a school gets even only one candidate from an ad, that person is going to spend a lot of money at their school.

Content Strategy for LinkedIn Ads

Think of your LinkedIn ads as a source of creating initial contact with potential clients. And just like when reaching out to people through messaging, you should use your ads to provide value to your customer before asking them for anything. Don't send out messages that directly ask people to call you or buy your service. You must begin by providing value to foster a connection and build up loyalty with people to demonstrate that you actually know what you're talking about. Provide potential customers with information that solves a problem or gives them insight on how to solve specific problems. With that strategy, you earn credibility and trust, which helps you move on to the next steps.

Again, LinkedIn ads are expensive, so you want to align with buyers' needs right away, which is difficult because oftentimes people don't know a lot about your business (people like this are referred to as "cold traffic" for those who speak marketing). Wilcox's team approaches this by introducing cold traffic to valuable offers that can make their jobs easier. It's a form of programmatic advertising where you offer your client something of extreme value in exchange for their email address or other pertinent information. By giving them valuable information at the onset you build credibility and trust.

Also, just like on the Facebook platform, you want to create ads that people click on because it helps lower your cost in the auction. When you have a great piece of content that gets a really high click-through rate, you'll have a better quality or relevancy score. Wilcox says that with a high relevancy score on LinkedIn, your cost per click can drop 20 or 30 cents, so the quality of your content is extremely important.

You need to give your audience something that's interesting enough to get clicked on. LinkedIn really values their community and won't push poor content. If people don't resonate with what you put out, they'll shut your ad off or cut down the amount of people that it's exposed to. If you have a great piece of content that people do engage with, on the other hand, LinkedIn will keep pushing it out.

Advertising Titles Are Important

Wilcox explains that the title of your content (or what we called headline in chapter four) is extremely important. The reason people interact with content, or provide their email address in exchange for downloading something, is because they think it will be of value. If your title is good enough to get people to want to learn more about your product, or sparks their interest in any way, then even if they don't read the rest of the article you'll still get a higher conversion rate.

A/B Test and Hypersegment Your Audience

As with all the social media platforms we've discussed, testing is a critical part of the equation in learning, experimenting, and figuring out the best way to engage with your intended audience and maximizing your marketing budget. The most important component to test is how the different segments of your target audience respond. This helps you understand how your message or offering resonates with various people within an organization.

Wilcox says that the best approach is to test specific job titles so you can measure and learn about the types of messages that are most effective for different roles. Each role in a company has specific motivations and job responsibilities, which alter the most effective way for you to communicate. For example, if a client comes to him and says, "We can sell our products to anyone in marketing," he will turn that into separate campaigns. He'll segment out marketing directors, marketing VPs, and CMOs. He'll launch the same content, in separate campaigns, to each targeted audience so he can learn how CMOs interact with the content versus how managers interact with it.

Wilcox adds that job titles can affect the way people act in regard to their click and conversion behaviors. The most sophisticated marketing teams in the business-to-business space know this and track every step of a lead. They study behaviors of qualified leads and figure out what loses or closes a deal. If you track behaviors all the way through the process, fascinating insights can come to light.

Perhaps you'll discover that CMOs are high to convert but then really hard to get on the phone; or that managers are easier to get hold of but are less likely to convert. (Keep in mind that these are just examples—you'll have to test to learn what's true about your audience and prospective clients. There are no shortcuts in this process.)

And after analyzing your data, you may discover that although you thought you'd rather have CMOs using your product, perhaps it's more realistic to target managers for a higher return on your investment. But you won't know unless you separate your audiences out and test them. Essentially, you may have a general assumption going in, but you should test that assumption before you put all your money in one direction.

After Wilcox has figured out which audiences are best to target, he starts looking at image size, introduction word length, and characters in the headline. Each of those aspects has a different level of importance. The image in the ad is really important because if people see the same image two or three times in their news feed they'll permanently ignore it. Wilcox explains that it's crucial to change up the image to keep an ad looking fresh so that click-through rates (CTRs) don't drop over time. He also knows that introductions are super important to test because it's what people read to see if your ad is worth clicking on.

Retargeting Ads on Other Platforms

As six to nine dollars a click for traffic is really expensive, you've got to make the most of your ads. Retargeting can help bring initial traffic you receive back at a cheaper price. Wilcox's team will often retarget ads on other platforms. LinkedIn does have its own form of retargeting, but Wilcox shares that the results are pretty weak due to people not spending as much time on LinkedIn as they do on other platforms. Usually they only come back once a week to check in. Retargeting requires being in front of your audience and staying on the radar, and LinkedIn just doesn't have that inventory. With Facebook ads, on the other hand, you're in front of people whenever they're on social media, either on Facebook or Instagram. And with Google AdWords, you are in front of them wherever they are on the web with the Google Display Network (GDN). So if you want to retarget traffic, your dream game is going to be Facebook ads and Google AdWords.

You can capture a lead on LinkedIn and then take that lead generation information, such as their email, and upload it to the Facebook ad platform or AdWords platform to retarget those people.

This furthers your chance of a final conversion or sale and allows you to make the most efficient use of the traffic for which you paid.

Quick Tips and Recap

- LinkedIn is a great platform for B2B targeting, searching for jobs, and for reaching business-minded people.

- Your level of access to people on LinkedIn, including those that can buy your product or give you jobs, is only limited by your ability to reach out.

- When connecting with others on LinkedIn, find a way to provide value. Start with a compliment or something that builds a relationship first. Don't sell them your service or product; instead, offer unique value to them through your product or service.

- Share content on your feed that provides value and starts a conversation. Even simple updates, thoughts, and experiences help you stay at the forefront of people's minds.

- It's easier to go viral on LinkedIn than on many of the other business platforms because any social interaction (a like, comment, or share) allows your content to be seen by your network and your network's network.

- Because of the level of specificity, especially in the business-to-business space, the LinkedIn ad platform is one of the most expensive in social media. On average, clicks cost anywhere between about six and nine dollars.

- The type of people that really benefit from the LinkedIn ad platform include those with large revenue generating B2B deals, products, or services (i.e., $10K+); those who know the targeting specifics of their buyers within organizations; white-collar recruiting; and higher-education recruiting.

- Use your ads to build credibility and trust. Offer potential clients something of extreme value.
- A/B test and hypersegment your audience to learn more about them and the effectiveness of your content.
- It's vital to change the images you use in ads to keep them looking fresh.
- Titles and introductions in ads are important to test because they're what people read to see if your ad is worth clicking on.
- Retarget your ads on other platforms such as Facebook, Instagram, or Google AdWords to maximize your spend.

CHAPTER 12

STAYING POWER

Congratulations for making it this far! Now you have a wealth of information and tools to help you build your audience and syndicate your content to the world. But the journey doesn't stop there. I imagine that many of you are reading this because you have big dreams and goals that you're trying to make come true. It's not about spiraling up, exploding, and disappearing like a firework. It's about becoming a guiding star—an entity that people search for again and again.

You need to become a brand, a name that people know and trust. Joivan Wade agrees that the most essential way to make a brand persist is by being trustworthy. Trust is at the core of everything. People need to know what you stand for, what your values are, what drives you—the mind-set behind how you create products and services. So let's examine how you can create staying power, relevance, and credibility to build a long-lasting and powerful brand.

It's Possible

First, you need to know that becoming a relevant household name is possible. Dream big! Prince Ea explains that a pilot will often take a route that's north of the destination; if he flies straight, he'll land lower than where he wants to go. He explains that this is a good analogy for work and life. If we're too realistic, we wind up pessimistic. But if we shoot for the moon, we wind up among the stars (exactly where we want to go). Famous hockey player Wayne Gretzky always said, "I never skate to where the puck is; I skate to where the puck is going to be."[1]

Go beyond what you think is possible. Envision something greater than that which you think you can achieve. Prince Ea says that he wants to shake up the world. You don't have to know how to do it, but you need to know that it's possible. Too many people get trapped because they don't believe in their abilities.

He also adds that personal growth must happen before you can have professional success. When you understand who you are, you're in a position to give your gift to the world. And you can't give something you don't have, which is why self-improvement and self-understanding are so important.

Focus on Who You Are

Everyone has a gift to give to the world. To find it, stay still, listen to your intuition, and know that you are complete as you are. Keep

---

[1] "Total Quality Leadership in a Changing World," 35th NACDA Convention, Orlando, Florida, June 11–14, 2000, http://www.nacda.com/convention/proceedings/2000/00leadership.html.

looking inside and ask yourself what makes you unique, why you're here, and what you have to offer.

Prince Ea offers the following questions to discover more about yourself, which can be applied to building your brand:

1. Why am I on the planet?
2. What can I give others?
3. What makes me happy?
4. If I had five years to live, what would I do?
5. If I had one year to live and knew that whatever I chose to do was guaranteed to succeed, what would I do?

Answering the above questions can really help you understand what you are here to do, help you believe it's possible, and help you have more follow-through in your work and in building your brand.

Nate Morley, founder of Works Collective and one of the top brand strategists in the United States, has worked as a group creative director at some of the best agencies in the world, including 72andSunny and Deutsch Los Angeles. He's also worked in global brand marketing at Nike and as the CMO at both Skullcandy and DC Shoes. At DC Shoes, Morley helped pioneer a new kind of branded content—the iconic Gymkhana series of films that have been viewed well over 500 million times. Gymkhana Three alone has been watched 65 million times with no paid support.

Morley says that when building a brand, there's a difference between who you are and what you do. "Most people think of Nike as a shoe company, but they're not," he said. "Nike is a performance company that makes shoes as a way to inspire and enable human performance. The expression of performance (shoes) has changed dramatically over the last forty years, but who they are as a brand has not. Nike started as a performance company, and that's who they are today, and who they will be in the future."

Creating a brand is hard. There are lots of shoe companies, but there is only one Nike.

Morley says that once you truly know who you are, you can do lots of different things and appeal to lots of different people. He applies this approach to his work with companies at all stages. "Most start-ups are hyper-focused on building a product and getting to market—and that's a good thing," he continued. "But there comes a time when a company needs to tell the story of who they are rather than what they make or do. What you make or do is an expression of who you are as a brand."

Chatbooks is a start-up that prints photo books from your camera roll and social media accounts. As a member of the advisory board, Morley helped Chatbooks realize that they're not a book-printing company—they're a "hold on to what matters" company that exists to inspire and enable people to hold on to and preserve the moments and people that matter most. The way they do that is by printing books, but that's not who they are at their core. Morley explains, "This approach will allow Chatbooks to evolve their product and service if they choose to without changing who they are as a brand."

Becoming a brand also helps you last in a changing world. For example, if you're a processing company that makes the world's best processor, but that's all you do, then the second someone else makes a better processor your company ceases to matter. That's why the best companies in the world use advertising to sell products as an expression of who they are as a brand. The best brands know how important it is to use resources exclusively for brand building.

Morley developed several campaigns for Target that didn't feature products at all. They purpose of the campaigns were simply to help people feel that Target is fashionable, cool, accessible, and fun. Most of the items Target sells can be purchased anywhere, but people want to buy from a brand they love.

Stand for Something Bigger

Journalist Katie Couric believes that people who learn how to combine the power of technology and storytelling will be the most successful long term. The possibilities are endless, but the competition for attention is more intense than ever before. The challenge is to get attention while staying true to your principles. Also, you need to have a strategy; otherwise you'll just have great content that no one sees.

Influencers must care about the world around them, not just about promoting new products or services. People must become brands in and of themselves that stand for something bigger. Couric feels that this is what truly increases the amplification of messages.

Build a Brand Around You

Phil Ranta of Studio71 says that one of his company's areas of focus is building brands around their creators so they have a safety net for a long career. In entertainment it's very rare that a celebrity enjoys longevity doing only one thing, especially in Ranta's industry where he works primarily with a youth audience. Generally younger people want to interact with others in their same age bracket. So he tries to ensure that once his clients go beyond that age bracket they still maintain an audience.

To stay relevant, it's important to build a brand around you—that way you mean more than simply the content you create right now. Rhett & Link (whom we discussed in the YouTube chapter) are a great example of people who have done this. After creating the hugely popular "Good Mythical Morning," they started the "Good Mythical Crew," which is focused on the people who work on their morning show. Not only are Rhett & Link personalities unto themselves, but they're also introducing their fans to a whole bunch of other people so they can continue to grow. Now they have fifteen personalities under their brand that everyone loves. It's always smart to evolve beyond being the only creator.

Use Multiple Channels

Chris Williams of pocket.watch explains that having reach isn't the same as having a brand. Getting a million followers on Facebook or getting fifty thousand views on a video doesn't mean you have a brand. Even eight hundred million views a month doesn't guarantee name recognition.

To turn a large number of followers into a brand, Williams recommends reaching people in multiple places. He thinks that YouTube star Jake Paul has transcended his digital brand because he went on the Disney Channel show "Bizaarvark." He didn't do it for the money—he did it because he knew that it would build his brand by getting out on more platforms. When people start seeing you in multiple places, you start building your brand. If, on the other hand, they associate you with a single platform, it's usually not enough.

Ray Chan of 9GAG agrees and says that your goal is to build a solid brand as you gain new users. Educate them and get them up to speed on what the brand is about. Let them know that you're on other channels so that they can engage with you in multiple ways.

Create Your Opportunities

Wade decided to create his own comedy show because although he wanted to walk into the BBC and Comedy Central to get a deal after graduating from theater school, he knew this wasn't realistic. Instead, he took the creative control into his own hands and made a show that he distributed online himself. By doing so he created a proof of concept—he had social proof in big numbers by getting the content seen online. Because his content performed extremely well it gave him validation and credibility to later go into big networks and get big deals.

He explains that you have to prove to the large channels that your concept will work. "Create your own buzz and the bees will follow," says Wade. When you create something for yourself, everyone else starts to show up—there's an influx and flurry of people that will get behind you and your ideas.

Wade got millions of views on his digital skits and shows before he went to the BBC and showed them that what he created was working. They gave him a show. He feels that anyone starting their own brand should take it into their own hands. No one owes you anything, so work hard to make your opportunities yourself.

Create a Strong Feeling of Connection

David Oh of FabFitFun explains that you need to be committed to and value your relationship with customers or fans. Staying power is achieved through maintaining a strong relationship with your audience. Building a million followers doesn't mean anything if you don't maintain a relationship and a connection with them.

You can foster a better connection by responding to and engaging with people who comment on your posts—it creates a connection to your company that people feel is genuine. FabFitFun has a forum where customers can ask whatever they want and Oh goes there himself to talk to customers. This has created a lot of value for the company. Oh explains that lots of brands seem afraid to do it, but he knows that the best entrepreneurs, including Steve Jobs and Bill Gates, have gone online and engaged.

He also adds that the greatest critiques come from your friends. If you treat your fans like friends they'll probably give you some good insight and advice. They might tell you what they like best about your company or page and help you improve over time.

No Secret to Success

Chan explains that you can't force success with so-called hacks or tricks, like looking at the time of day you post or by leveraging popular hashtags. Most users are intelligent and if they go to a hashtag and see content that's irrelevant, they won't follow your account. Hacks may help a little at the beginning, but the secret sauce of success is very straightforward—create the best experience on your platform for the users.

Chan explains that he learned a lot about this process by observing the movies he likes. He noticed that Marvel comics have tons of superhero movies that are very popular. Because of this, DC Comics tried to replicate Marvel's model. But when you look at box office sales, DC Comics' movies don't do as well as Marvel's movies. He learned that that is because the key element isn't the superhero itself. When you look deeper, the Marvel movies combine extremely funny parts mixed with heartfelt moments dealing with family issues and personal relationships. DC movies usually lack those aspects. DC tried to use a hack—the popularity of superheroes—when the secret was actually just great content that connects with people's emotions.

Adapt to Changing Platforms by Testing and Learning

Chan feels that being good at social media is hard because you have to excel and remain relevant even while the landscape and the social media platforms are constantly changing. New platforms emerge every few years and it keeps you working hard to adapt.

Wade agrees that there's constant volatility and that you need a way of navigating through those changes, which is exactly what building a brand helps you do. Brand building is one of the ways in which you can deal with the short-term ups and downs of consumer behavior changes or cultural shifts and societal pressures.

Chan thinks that a big contributing factor to his continuous success is that his team is constantly learning and testing to figure out

new ways to improve. The core principles about storytelling, entertaining, and engaging people through content have stayed the same,
but the constant learning, testing, and iteration bears on how you
package that content in a specific format for each platform.

For example, Facebook just announced a major change is coming to its news feed—it will focus on showing more content from
family and friends rather than from brands and media companies.[2]
This makes my strategy of leveraging the advertising platform even
more important to stay relevant on this channel. A lot of companies
will struggle if they don't see the value in using paid media to be
seen. Organic marketing for brands and media companies on Facebook will now be more difficult than before.

One (but not the only) way to adapt to this change is by leveraging the advertising strategies provided in this book and by having
integrity and creativity in the content offered. If your content isn't
highly shareable, then it absolutely won't be seen. This change is just
one example of how social media requires you to work hard and
constantly keep your strategies up-to-date.

Go for It

Everyone is given a purpose and a talent that helps him or her fulfill
that purpose. You can create a company and leverage any skill. Just
figure out how you can provide value to others. Follow your gut. If

---

[2] Kurt Wagner, "Facebook Is Making a Major Change to the News Feed
That Will Show You More Content from Friends and Family and Less from
Publishers," *Recode*, January 11, 2018, https://www.recode
.net/2018/1/11/16881160/facebook-mark-zuckerberg-news-feed-algorithm
-content-video-friends-family-media-publishers.

you have a dream, something you know you can't live without, then why would you stop pursuing it? The only way you can lose is if you quit.

Wade urges you to live your most authentic and best life. There's no reason you can't experience complete bliss. If you have a voice inside you that says, "I love doing this and I want to do it for the rest of my life," then don't let anything stop you. Even if you never "make it," the pursuit of a dream is more interesting than living a complacent life doing something you dislike.

Wade reminds us that you only live once. Take your one life and do something that makes you happy. Do everything in your power to make your dream a reality. If you don't build your dream, someone will hire you to build theirs.

Jonathan Skogmo of Jukin Media reminds entrepreneurs that success is not a race; it's a marathon. Just because you're not on a rocket ship doesn't mean you're not growing. And just because you were on a rocket ship at one point doesn't mean it will last forever because everyone runs out of fuel. He urges you to take your time, don't rush into things, and test all components of your business until you find the winning combination.

Get something out there, test and learn from it, and repeat what succeeded. You're in this for the long haul. Don't play the short game; play the long game. Wade reminds us that patience is paramount, something he feels most people don't appreciate. To have lasting significance you need to start today but wait for small successes over time. When you do something small but consistently it has a mass effect.

Start with one video or piece of content every other day, and then one video every day. With passion and time, you'll build something with value. A year from now, you'll be in a place you never would have thought imaginable. Start today and live your dreams.

Quick Tips and Recap

- Shoot for the moon.
- Understand who you are so you can give your gift to the world.
- Building a brand gives you a safety net for a longer career.
- Get on multiple platforms to build your brand.
- There's a difference between who you are and what you do. Focus on who you are for lasting success.
- Be trustworthy. Trust is at the core of everything.
- Build strong relationships with your customers; treat your fans like friends.
- Create the best experience on your platform for the users.
- Adapt to changing platforms by testing and learning.
- Create your own opportunities. If you create your own buzz, the bees will follow.
- The only way you can fail is if you quit.
- Do everything in your power to make your dream a reality.
- Take your time. Don't rush into things. Remember to test.
- Be patient.
- Start today and live your dreams.

ACKNOWLEDGMENTS

First of all, I'd like to thank my literary agent, Bill Gladstone, without whom this book wouldn't be possible. Bill, it's truly momentous that someone with your stature, having represented more than $5 billion dollars' worth of book sales, has taken the time to shepherd this project and my career as an author. Thank you for the continuous support and I look forward to working with you on future books.

Latham Arneson, thank you for being such a great friend. I always loved working with you at Paramount Pictures, especially when we had our deep and meaningful conversations about how to achieve maximum results for all of the movies we worked on. I look forward to continuing these conversations with you. Thanks again for being a part of this book.

To Erick Brownstein, I truly appreciate all the insight and guidance you've given me over the years. It's been amazing to see how much you've achieved in even the short amount of time that we've known each other. What your team does at Shareability is truly extraordinary—you were kind enough to offer valuable insight to the readers of this book on how to create more significant and powerful content.

Eamonn Carey, thank you for all of the inspirational conversations we have had over the years, especially when discussing the global picture of digital and business. Over the last ten years, I've learned a tremendous amount from the information you've shared with me.

Thank you Ray Chan of 9GAG; I really appreciate the time you took to share your wisdom for this book. There's no doubt in my mind about why 9GAG has been so successful. The many important lessons you provided in this book can help foster anyone's growth trajectory and social strategy.

To Ken Cheng, thank you for being such a great friend and collaborator over the years. It's always been exciting to discuss different concepts, strategies, and business models with you.

Katie Couric, thank you so much. Working with you the past three years has been outstanding—a true honor and pleasure. It's always fun to collaborate in the creation of compelling interviews and I look forward to continuing our work together. Additionally, I look forward to seeing the transformative content you'll produce in the coming years.

Thank you, Julius Dien, for taking the time for the interview at Web Summit. The level of growth you've generated is truly remarkable. This premise of this book started with achieving a million followers in thirty days, but you took it to the next level by generating 15 million followers in 15 months. Your content's continuous growth and virality is unmatched in my eyes.

To Pedro D. Flores, it's been amazing to know you over the years and hard to believe that it was ten years ago that we created one of the first ever influencer campaigns on YouTube (around the movie *Crank* with Jason Statham). It's always fun to watch the creativity and content you produce—you're one of the true original YouTube creators.

Tim Greenberg, thank you for taking the time to be a part of this book. I've always learned a tremendous amount from your incredibly innovative approach to fostering a global community around the World Surf League.

Thank you, Phil Ranta. Our meetings have always been motivating—even way back in the early days when you worked at Fullscreen. What you've achieved thus far in this industry is phenomenal. I continually learn from you and I want you to know that everything you share is truly appreciated.

To Jon Jashni, thank you for your eloquence. You're one of the most intelligent people I've met in the entertainment industry and every word that comes out of your mouth is like poetry. I'd also like to thank you for your continuous guidance and the deep conversations we have, not just about digital and the entertainment industry but also about life in general.

Mike Jurkovac, thank you. It's been incredible to work together over the past eight years, starting with our collaborations on Fashion Trust to Adriana Lima to now VAST. I really appreciate our collaborations and look forward to developing more innovative projects together.

Thank you, Jeff King. Your teachings about the Process Communication Model (PCM) have been transformative in my life. I'm grateful for all the support and guidance. I love our conversations about communication and how it not only impacts business, content, and social but also our daily lives. PCM and your presence in my life and career have been greatly significant.

To Rob Moran, thank you for your friendship and continuous guidance. It's been wonderful to work with you the past few years and I look forward to collaborating and working together in the near future.

Nate Morley, your intelligence and experience in branding are unmatched in my eyes. I see branding as one of the most important and critical factors for long-lasting growth. Whether working with Nike, Skull Candy, or DC Shoes, you always find the most innovative ways to create compelling content that engages and impacts the target audience. Thank you for the knowledge you provide in every conversation we have.

Thank you for your contribution, David Oh. I tell people that you are the smartest internet marketer I've ever met. Your level of expertise, experience, and insight is truly unmatched. I learn a tremendous amount every time we talk, and I'm always amazed by the growth you achieve in all the companies you've built over the years. The impressive growth that FabFitFun has achieved cannot be attributed to luck, but to your insight and experience. I look forward to collaborating with you on future projects.

To Kario Salem, your friendship means a great deal to me. I always enjoy our conversations and look forward to watching your continuous growth, not only as a screenwriter but also as a musician. Working and collaborating with you on social campaigns for your music is fun and exciting.

Jonathan Skogmo, thank you. It's unbelievable that we moved out to LA together from Chicago and that you formed Jukin Media out of the apartment in which we lived at that time. Seeing your personal growth and that of your company is astounding. When I walk through your office I'm inspired by and proud of your company's accomplishments. We've come a long way together.

Thank you, Joivan Wade. Our conversations are truly wonderful. To meet someone from the other side of the world that has the same mind-set and goals as I do is really exciting. I always love your inspirational insights and I look forward to collaborating with you in the future.

To AJ Wilcox, thank you. What you've achieved on LinkedIn is remarkable. Managing more than $100 million of spend on the LinkedIn platform is a true testament to your level of expertise and knowledge. I've always enjoyed our conversations and I look forward to future collaborations.

Chris Williams, you're truly a sensational person. I remember the first time we met, when you were still the chief community officer of Maker Studios—I knew then that you were one of the smartest guys in digital. Your insights are invaluable to this book and to my own knowledge and growth. The growth and scale that you've achieved in such a short period of time with your new company, pocket.watch, is truly inspiring.

I'd like to thank Prince Ea. Thank you for taking the time to share your wisdom in our interview for this book and for influencing me with your inspirational and motivational approach to producing digital content. What you've achieved in such a short period of time is truly remarkable. By creating some of the most viral videos on the planet, you've taught us all how to create great social content and how to live positive and impactful lives.

Knowledge and insight was gleaned from all of the interviewees who dedicated their time to this project, many of whom were previously mentioned. I'm truly grateful for all of your time and participation. A special thanks to everyone who participated, including Christy Ahni, Anthony Arron, Chris Barton, and Chris Carmichael.

To the team at BenBella, thank you for your dedication to refining the content of this book and for preparing it to go to market. A sincere thanks to all the team, and especially to Glenn Yeffeth, Vy Tran, Sarah Avinger, Adrienne Lang, and Jennifer Canzoneri.

Thank you to the brilliant members of my team at OPTin.tv. Our own growth would not be possible without your continuous hard work and dedication. A special salute to Shant Yegparian, Dave Siedler, Strahil Hadzhiev, and Mike Seager.

Tara Rose Gladstone, thank you so much for all of your support in generating this book; it definitely wouldn't have been possible without you. It's been a remarkable process to work with you—there's been highs and lows, but I think the final product really turned out outstanding because of your effort, your dedication, and the time you've put in. I truly appreciate it and look forward to collaborating with you on future projects.

And last, but certainly not least, I'd like to thank Geyer Kosinski, Gary Lucchesi, Antony Randall, Pete Wilson, Brian McNelis, and Richard Wright for their mentorship over the years. I really appreciate your continual guidance and support.

INDEX

ABOUT THE AUTHOR

BRENDAN KANE is a business and digital strategist for Fortune 500 corporations, brands, and celebrities. He thrives on helping his clients systematically find and engage new audiences that reward relevant content, products, and services with their attention and spend. Brendan's greatest strength is unlocking value. He transforms complexity into simplicity

© Micheal John Seager

with tools and methods that amplify growth and enable execution.

Starting his career at Lakeshore Entertainment, Brendan oversaw all aspects of their interactive media strategy. He worked on sixteen films that generated a worldwide gross of $685 million and pioneered the first ever influencer campaign to effectively promote Lakeshore's movies.

Brendan went on to build applications and platforms for celebrity clients such as Taylor Swift, Rihanna, Xzibit, Charles Barkley, Michael Strahan, supermodel Adriana Lima, and pro skateboarder Ryan Sheckler. He also served as vice president of digital for Paramount Pictures and helped scale one of the largest social optimization firms in the world, that works with brands such as Disney, Fox, NBC, Netflix, Xbox, LinkedIn, and many notable Fortune 100 companies.

Contact Brendan at b@optin.tv.